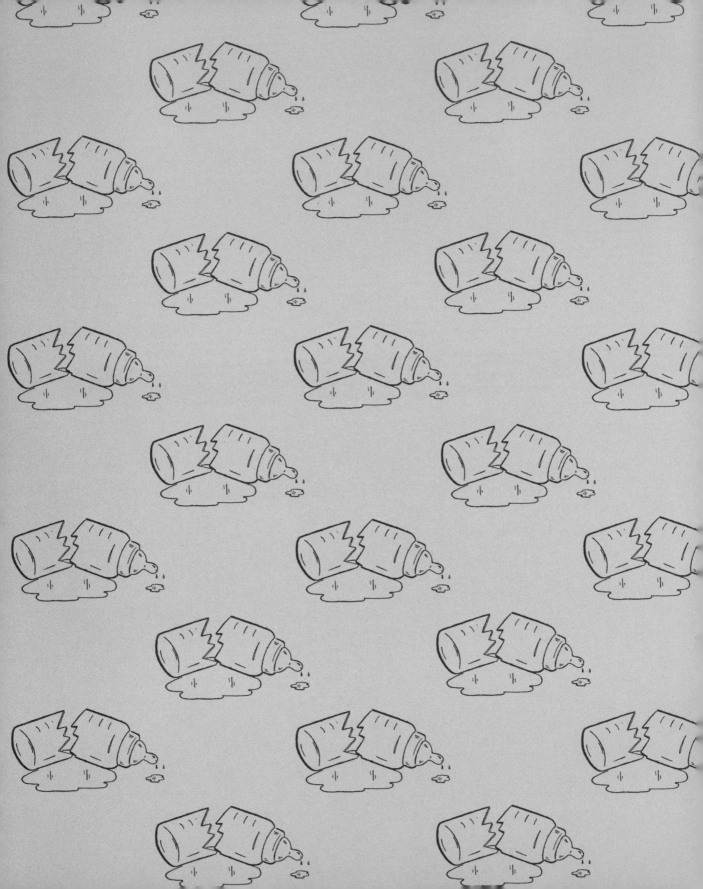

MAMA TRIED

MAMA TRIED

DISPATCHES FROM THE SEAMY
UNDERBELLY OF MODERN PARENTING

EMILY FLAKE

Grand Central Publishing
New York   Boston

Grand Central Publishing
Hachette Book Group
1290 Avenue of the Americas
New York, NY 10104

www.HachetteBookGroup.com

Q-MA

Printed in the United States of America

First Edition: October 2015
10 9 8 7 6 5 4 3 2 1

Grand Central Publishing is a division of Hachette Book Group, Inc.
The Grand Central Publishing name and logo is a trademark of Hachette Book Group, Inc.

The Hachette Speakers Bureau provides a wide range of authors for speaking events. To find out more, go to www.hachettespeakersbureau.com or call (866) 376-6591.

The publisher is not responsible for websites (or their content) that are not owned by the publisher.

Library of Congress Cataloging-in-Publication Data has been applied for.
ISBN: 978-1-455-55823-0

This one's for you, Scratchpad.

ACKNOWLEDGMENTS

Thank you to my stellar and lovely agent, Meg Thompson, and to Ben Greenberg, Maddie Caldwell, and Liz Connor at Grand Central Publishing, for everything from the conception of this project to its birth. Thank you to Tim Kreider for introducing me to Meg in the first place. Thank you to Lana and the staff of Little Stars for looking after the child while her daddy and I worked. Thank you to my own parents, who had to do all of this without the Internet. Thank you to the Summer '12 Mamas, a true lifesaver of a group. Thank you to Annie, Gaylord, and Lizzy, and special thanks to Annie's porch. Thank you to Tug's loving and beloved godparents, Pat and Jackie. Thank you to Ed and Deborah, as always, forever. Thank you to my awesome sister, Melissa. And my huge, daily, thunderous gratitude to and for my husband and daughter, John and Tug, Fat Man and Little Bear, Mr. Boombatty and the Tugster. I love you so much.

MAMA TRIED

INTRODUCTION

We* live in weird times for parenting. More specifically, we live in pro-
foundly *spazzy* times for parenting. The Internet provides us with a
million little rabbit holes to fall down every day, researching things like
vaccines, or the hazards of BPA lining, or Magda Gerber's "respect-based"
approach vs. Attachment Parenting. Never before in human history has
it been so possible to convince yourself you're doing everything horribly,
horribly wrong. We are all freaking the fuck out, all the time.

The echo chamber of parental fear is vast, and the air in there can
carry an unpleasant odor of smug martyrdom—if you're not worried to
death all the time, it's because you're not a good enough parent. Compet-
itive anxiety figures heavily in the zeitgeist—of course, I live in Brooklyn.

---

* There's not much getting around the fact that by "we" I mean middle-class folks who
went to college and what have you, who put off having babies to get a career going
or because we still had a lot of drinking to do or both. My sister had her first child at
seventeen and then put herself through college; her experience of motherhood was
less about Sophie the Giraffe teethers and Mothers' Groups and more about trying not
to go insane while waiting tables at Friendly's and going to nursing school. I am going
to be over here making Sophie jokes and feeling like a pussy.

Not in, but quite near to, Park Slope, which is ground zero for all manner of parenting craziness. Not only is it ripe—so deliciously, floridly ripe!—for satire, you also *have* to laugh at it, because if you don't, you will drop dead of a heart attack or from the peanut allergy your kid gave you. It is my hope that this book will provide you with a chuckle, and perhaps help deflate the giant balloon of anxiety that lives in your belly or throat or wherever you keep yours. It can be lonely, this parenting gig. It helps to be reminded that the boat is huge, and there are a lot of us in it.

I try my best to keep all that worry and anxiety at bay (arguably to the point of skewing dangerously laissez-faire, and possibly because I am very lazy). A pregnant friend asked my advice about juggling work and baby, and all I could come up with was "Try to embrace the fact that you're gonna be half-assing everything for a while." And yet, despite my best intentions, I am not immune to panic: as a small baby, for instance, my daughter was plagued with dry, itchy, eczema-prone skin. I spent countless hours in a rabbit hole of skin-issues blogs and bought hundreds of dollars' worth of creams, lotions, and unguents of every kind. I called our pediatrician, long-distance, from *Europe*, because the baby was *scratching*. I had found my crazy. As it happens, switching her to a hypoallergenic formula that was twice as expensive as the regular kind and smelled like Cheetos-and-feet cleared it all up. We tried her on cow's milk at twelve months—I was getting dead sick of that Cheetos-feet smell. She guzzles it down happily and not a rash in sight. But the episode stands as a reminder that panic can also seem silly until it's, you know, *your* panic.

This book is not a parenting manual. I do not have any particularly sage advice for parents; my daughter is, as I write this, still quite young. The ways in which my husband and I have damaged her have yet to manifest in any noticeable sense. We will make mistakes. Hopefully we'll get some things right. Someday, God willing, she will be an adult. I very much hope she never has to be a general in the human rebel army in the great robot wars once the Internet becomes sentient and tries to kill us all, because all this foofaraw about child-led weaning and whether or not cry-it-out is cruel is going to look awfully stupid. That said, the point of this book is to spelunk around in the dark places, where we keep our fear, our petty jealousy, our ineptitude, our fatigue—to go there, find these things, and make fun of them. If it can help a mom breastfeeding at 4 AM feel a little comic relief or provide a dad with a moment of levity when he's on the toilet trying desperately to finish taking a shit before his daughter wakes up, I will feel like I have done some small measure of good in the world.

TRYING TO CONCEIVE, SORTA

I went off the Pill on—rather, I should say "for"—my thirty-fourth birth-day. I'd been rolling around with the hazy idea of "I want a kid someday" since forever, but as I hit my midthirties it was beginning to dawn on me that "someday" might mean "never" if I dillydallied too long. I took the sentiment "If everyone waited until they were ready to have kids, nobody would ever have them" to heart; it meshed well with my general tendency toward seat-of-the-pantsism. My husband is ten years my senior and had never been much of a kid person. I managed to talk him into getting a cat, a creature who ultimately served as a gateway drug into procreation. "You didn't want a cat," I said, "but look how nice having one turned out." He grumbled, but he went along with it.

I went on the Pill shortly after I turned sixteen—that shakes out to my having been on one form or another of chemical birth control for over half my life. I had been trying to pre-vent my body from carrying a child for nearly as long as it had the ability to do so, so naturally I wondered: Did I even still know how to ovulate? Had all those eggs, tied up in storage for so long, gone bad? It is unfair that biology lays this burden—this use-it-or-lose-it bullshit—on the ladies, but, you know, you can't fight City Hall. I prepared myself for a long wait and some disappointment, and let the part of me that was still ambivalent about having children take comfort in the fact that hey, if it doesn't work, it doesn't work. We weren't *trying* to have children, we had just stopped actively preventing them from coming.

Much to my surprise, my body seemed to know what it was doing. I went off the Pill in June and got a positive pregnancy test in September. That pregnancy didn't take; I'd only known I was pregnant for four days when all of a sudden I wasn't anymore. The term is, apparently, "spontaneous abortion," which sounds much jauntier than the reality. I had hardly even had time to wrap my head around the fact that I couldn't smoke—my main memory of that very brief pregnancy is of feeling like I had removed myself from my own life for a second. I felt lost, a bit panicked, yet when it became clear that I had lost this whatever-it-was, I was disappointed. Not shattered, though. I carried on like normal.

I peed on a few sticks to see if I could gauge an optimal window, but according to the sticks my hormone levels weren't really spiking at all.

Maybe I didn't work so well after all, I thought. I began to worry that whatever had gone wrong with the first pregnancy was preventing me from conceiving a second time—maybe my eggs were all old and rot-

ten, unusable. I made an appointment with my OB-GYN for February 14 (nothing says Valentine's Day like having your feet in the stirrups) to have my equipment checked for defects. On February 10 I went out with my best lady friend; on February 11, more than a little hungover, I peed on a stick on a whim—I didn't really think I was pregnant.

Except, of course, I was. Sorry, baby! I didn't see you there, I hope I didn't get whiskey all over your DNA. I put the pack of cigarettes I'd bought the night before into the freezer, because this baby might take.

It took.

I'm not sure what we would have done if it *hadn't* taken. I felt very ambivalent about the idea of medically assisted pregnancy—as unsure as I was about having a child in the first place, I couldn't see myself having the determination to undergo all the various medical procedures involved. I have many friends who've had medically assisted pregnancies, from hormone shots to IVF to some truly spectacular feats of engineering involving donor eggs. That kind of wanting a child—that determination and dedication to childbearing—is not a thing I felt until I actually had one. Now that I have my daughter it feels weird to say it, but I had a hard time imagining I would have taken that long, hard, often heartbreaking, always expensive road for the sake of something that felt so abstract. I am not certain this bodes well for me as a mother—like, I'll do this, but not if it's gonna be some big pain in the ass—but Tug came through being infused with whiskey at six weeks gone well enough; she seems, thus far, reasonably equipped to handle my inadequacies as a mother and a person. Knock on wood.

Are You Ready for Children?

DO YOU THINK "CHILDPROOFING" MEANS FORTIFYING YOUR HOME AGAINST TODDLERS?

ARE YOU PRONE TO MAKING THESE KINDS OF STATEMENTS?

HOW HUNGOVER WERE YOU WHEN YOU TOOK THE TEST?

CAN YOU SAY "CHILD REARING" WITHOUT CRACKING UP LIKE A TWELVE-YEAR-OLD?

IS YOUR *Relationship* STRONG ENOUGH FOR KIDS?

Preparing the Vessel

Thank you for ordering Natural Horizons Fertility Formula Vitamin Powder. Here are some tips to help you prepare your body for its most important job: creating and sustaining life!

First, take a look at your habits. We'll assume you neither smoke nor drink to excess, because no woman who hopes to be a Vessel would desecrate her body in such a way. Our powder is a wonderful way to ensure that your body gets the nutrients it needs, but here are a few suggestions of foods that will help support your body in its fertility journey:

Dark, leafy greens

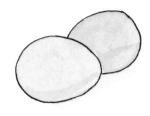

Eggs (organic, of course!)

Plant proteins, such as nuts and beans

Whole grains

Raw, red meat

Ovaries of a fertile mammal, preferably consumed within minutes of extraction

Of course, how you eat is as important as what you eat. Try to make meals a time of reflection and relaxation, and communion with your partner. Enjoy your food — be mindful as you eat, remembering that the nutrition you take in is helping your body prepare for its sacred role.

Upon arising in the morning, turn your face to the East. Before allowing a morsel of food to cross your lips, recite the Prayer of Obeisance to Aramazd (enclosed). Now you're ready to prepare your Vitamin Shake! Empty a vial into a crystal or stone goblet. Add four to five ounces of fresh, warm goat's blood. Mix with a silver spoon and drink in one gulp.

If you've been charting your menstrual cycle, you should have a good idea of when your most fertile days are. Make sure you and hubby get extra close during this time! When he comes to you, it should be in the guise of a satyr. The optimum time for conception is thirteen minutes past midnight. Have your attendants cover their faces with dark veils, preferably of leather. Chant the Invocation of Souls (enclosed) as your husband enters you, and carry on chanting it until he reaches his moment of crisis.

Think carefully about what kind of soul you wish to attract to your womb. The enclosed chart will help you arrange your bedroom furniture in such a way that your coupling will attract a fine, warlike soul. If you suspect your womb has attracted the soul of Natural Horizons founder Abe Rabinowitz, please drop us an email and we will happily send a representative to administer The Test.

If you and your baby pass/survive The Test, congratulations! You are the new CEO of Natural Horizons and Dark Lord of the Universe, respectively.

FIRST TRIMESTER: THE SICKENING

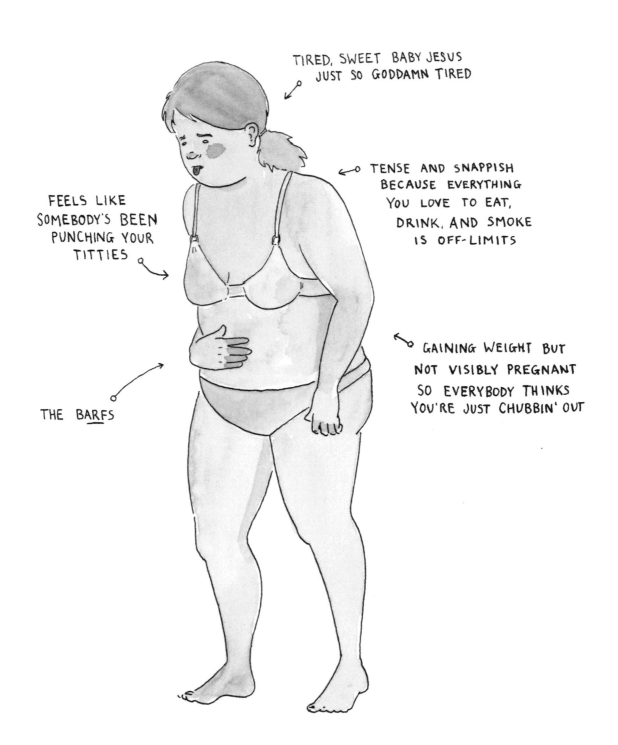

HAVING KIDS CHANGES YOU...

(PUKING HUNGOVER INTO A SINKFUL OF DIRTY DISHES)

... BUT NOT ALWAYS TH<u>A</u>T MUCH

NOT SAFE
DURING   PREGNANCY

SAFE DURING PREGNANCY

KALE*

SOFT CHEESE   FOREIGN CHEESE

CHEESE STEAK   VIGOROUS SEX   BIKE-RIDING

CAUTIOUS, TIMID SEX

HEAVY READING

HONEY   SUGAR

CHINESE FOOD

SAYING THE WORD "CIGARETTE"

ATMs

SUNSHINE   DRIVING

IMPURE MIASMAS

ANY MUSIC WITH UNUSUAL TIME SIGNATURES

"What to Expect"

CAN GO
FUCK
ITSELF

NON-ROM-COM FILM

DEPICTIONS OF PILL USE

MAN-MADE FABRICS

HEROIN

*USE WITH CAUTION

THAT TIME I GREW A BABY IN MY BODY

There's a spectrum of the pregnancy experience. At one extreme, you have the Earth-Goddess Mama, for whom pregnancy is a magical, spiritual experience. She feels deeply in touch with her body and the changes it's going though in order to bring new life into this world. At the other extreme, you have the ladies for whom pregnancy is a near-catastrophic event, rife with problems ranging from the annoying (swollen feet, weird itching) to the life-threatening (preeclampsia). She feels hijacked, usurped, her reliable body transformed by dark biological magic into a bloated, leaky vessel from which a squalling tomato will emerge demanding to be fed.

My own pregnancy occupied a pleasant neutral ground between the two. On one hand, I did not feel a magical connection to the Life Spirit nor to my fetus—in fact, I was highly skeptical that this thing in my belly was actually going to turn out to be a human child. Logically, I knew it would, but emotionally, I had my doubts. On the other hand, except for putting on more weight than was strictly necessary and developing feet that were practically spherical, I felt fine. My morning sickness took the form of a low-level, month-long hangover—nothing I couldn't handle, since I'd been handling hangovers for years. I never got heartburn, I never got gestational diabetes—it was all pretty unremarkable. Sometimes, a little too unremarkable: she was really *quiet* inside—no kicks to the ribs, no drumming of tiny fists against my internal organs. Some days, she was so quiet that I would eat something sugary or laden with caffeine and lie still, heart in mouth, waiting to see if she would move at all. But generally speaking, my body approached pregnancy with the phlegmatic efficiency of a draft horse.

WHATEVER.

Some women's pregnancies present as a joyous balloon, a big ol' bump on an otherwise normal frame; mine involved a general rounding of everything, a situation mainly of my own making. You could tell I was pregnant, but you could also be forgiven for thinking I had just gotten fat. I topped out at 215 pounds at 5'6" and the bother to my knees was enough to make me want to never weigh that much absent a pregnancy. It's tiring to be that heavy. I was not beset by any specific food cravings, but I developed a strong aversion to crab and lobster (a situation that has, blessedly, resolved since). I ate what I wanted, which was everything, and a lot of it. I was unreservedly gluttonous, reasoning that breastfeeding would take care of the weight. This turned out to be untrue.

Emotionally, what I mostly felt was a fascination with the weirdness of being pregnant. I felt a little special. I held strangers' eyes and smiled beatifically; I didn't feel like an earth-goddess, but I was not above being fussed over. I read pregnancy blogs and forums, feeling like I had joined a club, but also just a bit like a fraud—the words "I'm pregnant" never felt quite right coming out of my mouth. When I said them, I felt as though I were being overly dramatic—I mean, sure, they say there's a baby in there, but I'm not, like, *pregnant*-pregnant. Let's not get carried away. I believed in the baby for a full day after the twenty-week scan, where we learned her gender and she looked, for the first time, like a human child and not a flailing dinosaur bud. Twenty-four hours later, though, the whole thing reverted into the abstract until I gave birth (or, truth be told, a few weeks after that).

I thought I might feel like the baby was a beautiful commingling of my husband and me, from us, by us, part of us. But when I saw the tiny creature on the screen, it felt immediately like she was a discrete human being (or would be). I didn't feel a deep sense of her *belonging* to me so much as a profound sense of stewardship of her. She belonged to herself, but had been given to us for safekeeping. Perhaps it was a little magical after all.

SECOND TRIMESTER: THE SMUGGENING

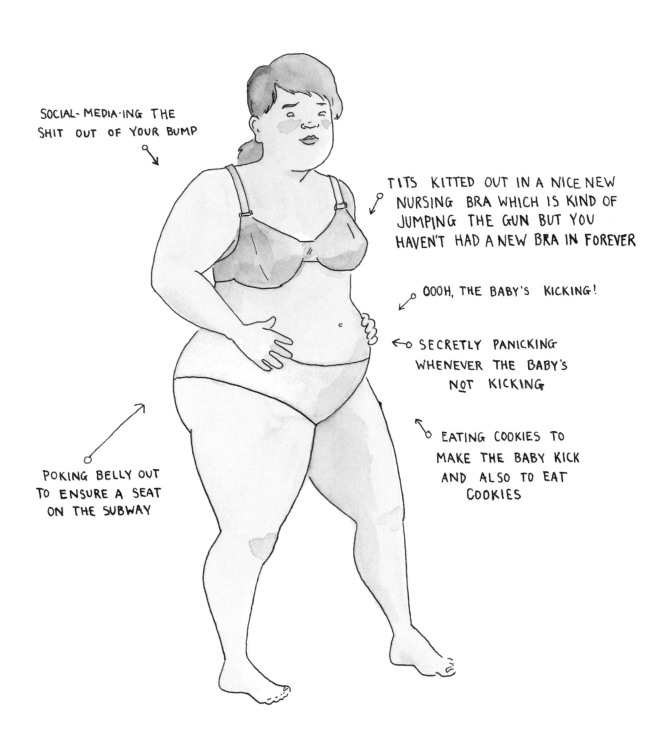

SOCIAL-MEDIA-ING THE SHIT OUT OF YOUR BUMP

TITS KITTED OUT IN A NICE NEW NURSING BRA WHICH IS KIND OF JUMPING THE GUN BUT YOU HAVEN'T HAD A NEW BRA IN FOREVER

OOOH, THE BABY'S KICKING!

SECRETLY PANICKING WHENEVER THE BABY'S NOT KICKING

POKING BELLY OUT TO ENSURE A SEAT ON THE SUBWAY

EATING COOKIES TO MAKE THE BABY KICK AND ALSO TO EAT COOKIES

(OR: I'M JUST GONNA BREASTFEED THIS ASS AWAY SO COOKIE ME, BITCH)

34 AND PREGNANT

My sister got pregnant when she was seventeen, delivering a ten-pound, six-ounce (!!) baby boy two weeks shy of her eighteenth birthday. Hers was the first newborn I'd ever really seen up close—I was thirteen at the time.

Her relationship with that baby's father went the way those usually do—after living with us for a while, they decamped to a cruddy apartment on the cruddy side of a cruddy town until things went to hell and she moved back in with us. She waitressed her way through nursing school and married a man with whom she had two more boys. They've since divorced, and she lives with her boyfriend in a big old farmhouse in Massachusetts. She is a postpartum nurse (and a certified lactation consultant, which was handy for me). I asked her once who her least favorite kind of patient was. "Oh, you know, older, professional moms who read too many parenting websites." "Like me?" I asked. "Ha!" she said. "Kind of! I mean, you're not a jerk, but you did have a doula."

My sister's and my experiences of pregnancy and child rearing are as different from each other as you're likely to see with two people from the same family. The announcement of her first pregnancy was met with white-hot anger (our mom) and gentle stoicism (our dad). The announcement of mine was met with a resounding "It's about goddamn time." My parents had been after me to get on the ball for years—and to that end, had been helping me out with health insurance in those pre-Obamacare days, since my main argument against having a child was that I couldn't afford the insurance myself. When I picked up the phone to tell them, I felt a slight twinge of spoiled rebellion—I didn't want them to know I'd Done What I Was Supposed to Do. I wanted to guard this information from them as jealously as I would have guarded my high school diary, or a note from a boyfriend. But if I didn't want to tell them, it certainly wasn't because I was terrified that I would be kicked out of the house.

My parents and my sister live in the same small town, and their lives are tangled up in each other's in a way that mine is not. My parents have had a much bigger role in my nephews' lives than they will in my daughter's. My life as a mother has a lot more choice in it than my sister's has; I get to choose who will mind my child when John and I can't and what adults she'll be around—in short, I've gotten to choose my support system. Obviously you can't take advantage of your friends the way you can your family, and John and I have to pay for our child care, but it still shakes down to my having the privilege of designing my life in a way that wasn't an option for her.

My adult life has been full of choice. I got to choose when to get pregnant, I got to choose a career, I got to choose to develop that career before I started a family. There are plenty of people who don't have these choices; I think the danger for those of us who do have them is that childbearing becomes another step in a curated life that you've let yourself think is important. This is an incredibly hypocritical thing to say, considering here I am writing a parenting memoir—but I'm not important, having a child is not an amazing feat, and my child, while extraordinarily important to and beloved by her parents, is not particularly special in the scheme of things. (Yet. Maybe she'll be president! Or a serial killer!) The world held no compunctions about letting my sister know she wasn't important when she walked around with her big Tragic Pregnant Teen belly, all crispy hair and eyeliner.

Nobody went out of their way to make her feel special, unless you count trying to make her feel especially ashamed. I, on the other hand, have been steeped in a culture designed to make me view my pregnancy and my child as amazing, an incredible journey, a wildly difficult and world-changing thing. Bullshit. I'm just another lady that had a goddamn kid, and so are you, and so is everybody else.

WEEK 13

CONGRATULATIONS! You're entering the "sweet spot" of pregnancy now - the second trimester, when your energy rises, your nausea abates, and you've more or less resigned yourself to this whole "having a baby" deal. A word to the wise: you'll probably start to show soon, so put down those cigarettes before some nosey Parker reads you the riot act!

By now, your baby is about the size of a chayote. Do you not know what a chayote is? God, the whole foodie revolution just sailed right over your pretty little head, didn't it? How about a kiwi? Ever seen a kiwi, chef? It's about that size, but hopefully not as hairy. Though, if the father's any indication, who knows, am I right? Wait, you do know who the father is, don't you?

By now, your baby looks like a cross between a comma with eyes and a mountain of crushing debt. And did you know it can p<u>ee</u>? Well, it can.

In fact, it's probably peeing ri<u>ght</u> n<u>ow</u>.

<u>Inside of you.</u>

If you're not feeling that second trimester energy rush, it's because your little monster is siphoning off all your bodily resources, like a tumor that's going to want to go to college someday.

You may also be experiencing food cravings and bouts of crippling depression. Why not assuage both by eating everything in sight?

Speaking of being fat, you may notice some changes in your physique. Your tits are over, aesthetically. Buy a punitively hideous bra and think about what you've done.

You're also likely to get stretch marks on them, as well as your belly and thighs. Try thinking of them as lightning bolts highlighting your least attractive parts. At least you won't get them on your face! Probably.

Now is a good time for your partner to practice hiding his disgust at your body, and to start dragging his dreams out behind the woodshed one by one to strangle them. The less he feels his life ever held possibility, the better for both of you, and for baby. While you're at it, have him strangle yours as well.

Doesn't that feel better?

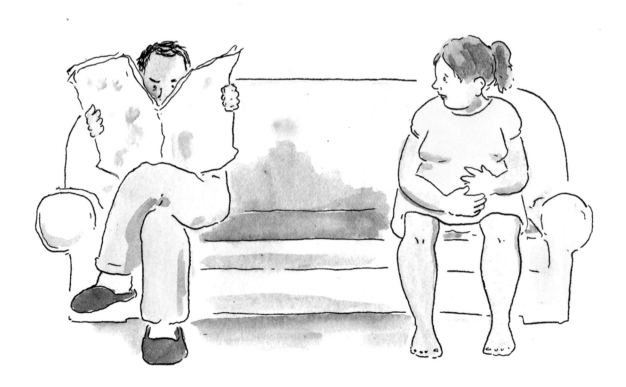

How do you feel about your OB-GYN? If you didn't go to at least twelve of them in your quest to find the woman who's going to be your Sherpa on this incredible journey, you haven't looked hard enough. "Competent" and "takes my insurance" are not sufficient criteria, not by a long shot. Have you started researching birthing centers yet? Or home births? The pros and cons of Attachment Parenting? Jesus, why don't you just whelp in the alley behind the dollar slice joint up the street? Maybe they'll toss you a free Coke.

Gimme a dollar and I'll be your doula.

But the most important thing to remember is this: the powerful, all-encompassing love you're going to feel when you look into your baby's face for the first time. You won't believe how amazing it is.

Unless, of course, your baby turns out to be some kind of terrible mutant. Then it will just feel weird. Good luck, Mama!

EPIGENETICS:
What Does It Mean For You?

As our understanding of how the genetic code upon which the human race is built expands and increases, we are coming to an exciting new frontier: epigenetics. You know what genes are—after all, you picked your spouse or sperm donor based on his apparent possession of "good" ones, based on the squareness of his jaw, the broadness of his shoulders, or the exhaustive details of his semen profile. But did you know that coiled deep within our cells lies a shadow DNA, a DNA that passes on the experiences and history of our entire background? That's epigenetics, and it's very important that you take the epigenetic profile of your mate into consideration when it comes time to procreate.

Here's how it works. Let's say—despite his sparkling eyes and world-class education—your partner's background includes immigrant forebears with a less-than-ideal history. Perhaps his great-grandmother grew up in a shtetl, never getting quite enough to eat. That experience of starving imprinted itself in her DNA! And thus it can be passed on to your baby, whose chances of starving to death are close to nil. But your baby's cells don't know they live in a world full of nutritious, organic food readily

delivered to your door via any number of websites, so they're going to tell your baby she could starve! Isn't that horrible?

Let's look at some other examples. Perhaps, somewhere in there, an ancestor was involved in the losing side of a genocide or forced relocation. Those ghastly memories will form part of your child's genetic makeup, which could be expressed in a number of unpleasant ways, from food hoarding to a tendency to form a rebel underground. Was your grandmother a smoker? It's OK to admit it; those were different times. But your grandmother's carelessness with her health could lead to problems for your child, such as obesity or delinquency. Did your father ever speak sharply to your mother? That experience could reverberate through your child's genetic code, causing him or her to have severe problems with conflict management. Taken together, these negative histories form what are known as "bummer strands" of genetic code.

So, how can you avoid passing on these "bummer strands" to your own children? Step one is to screen your potential mate very, very carefully.

Find out family habits in terms of drug use, education, and pop-culture consumption, going back as many generations as possible. Your mate may appear, on the surface, to be intelligent, hardworking, and healthy, but you'll never know the truth until you do your research—don't wait for the truth to out itself in the form of a child. Your best bet is to find a mate whose ancestors come from a population with no history of deprivation, war, or alcoholism. Studies show that such a mate can be found among the inhabitants of a small, isolated mountain village deep in the Caucasus. There are five such people of breeding age available.

However, securing access to this genetic gold may prove tricky. And even if you do, it hardly takes care of the problem of your own genetic history. All the careful screening in the word can't help the fact that your grandmother was exposed to plastics fumes through her entire childhood, thus virtually guaranteeing that your child will be ravaged by sensitivities to gluten, soy, and dairy. That's where CynoDyne Fetal Bots come in.

Our bots, introduced to the womb within five weeks of conception, will slowly, lovingly reshape your child's DNA to eliminate any "bummer strands" and replace them with "winner strands." They are carefully programmed to comb through millions of strands of code as your child knits together, identifying trouble spots such as ingrained fear response to German shepherds or a tendency toward fugue states. The bots will snip out this information and replace it with positive traits that will give your child advantages in business and social arenas. CynoDyne has gained access to the epigenetic material of such leading

lights as Bill Gates, Oprah Winfrey, and Machiavelli, and our bots are ready to incorporate that precious material into the cells of your unborn child—leaving out, of course, the information that leads to yo-yo dieting or a predilection for unflattering sweaters. The introduction of bots also provides you, the host, with an opportunity to get creative—would you like your child's cells to have the memory of flight? Or perhaps you'd like to go all out and have your child form actual wings! Anything is possible with

Intellectual property of CynoDyne.

our bots. It should go without saying that your* genetically enhanced child will have a definite edge as CynoDyne moves closer to Sentient Robotics, a field poised to transform our world to unprecedented wealth and productivity—no need for those bad shtetl-memories here! Tomorrow's world will offer challenges and opportunities unlike any other in human history. Now is your chance to create a *child* unlike any other in human history— a child who has been freed from the weight of the past is a child who can soar into the future. Contact your CynoDyne rep today!

---

* Any child resulting from a bot-assisted pregnancy becomes the intellectual property of CynoDyne Industries, Inc.

Some Kind of Bougie Things I Did When I Was Pregnant

1. I hired a doula. I felt weird about this. There is a smarmy, fancy-pants tang to the word "doula" that I find off-putting, and I wondered if perhaps it wasn't a ridiculous waste of money.

THE DOULA.

On the other hand, my OB-GYN, while certainly competent*, wasn't much for details. Throughout my pregnancy I never spent more than five minutes with her; we never discussed anything about the actual having of the baby. She seemed like she had a lot of other patients. I am

---

* Not a thing I can say about the doctor covering her patients when she went on her own maternity leave about halfway through my pregnancy. This guy listened for the heartbeat, and frowned, and said, "That doesn't seem right. I hear two heartbeats." Pause. "Oh, one must be yours." YOU THINK?

loath to make trouble. It seemed easier to just hire some lady to act as my Birth Sherpa.

I went to the website of a local Fancy Pregnancy studio—the kind of place that has a lot of baby yoga and mindful parenting classes. They offered a list of affiliated doulas ranked into tiers—the cheapest being the least experienced at $300, the most expensive being Wizard Doulas at $2400. Reasoning that my usual MO was to order the second-cheapest bottle of wine, I requested a doula from Tier Two. There was a questionnaire, so that you could list the qualities you'd like in your doula. "Sense of humor important," I wrote.

They matched me with a woman named Mollie who, to my relief, seemed like a reasonable person. She was funny, and smart, and didn't roll in with a whole lot of Goddess crap.

I did not have birth preferences, per se, beyond "get me and my baby out of this alive," but I did want someone

THE ANGEL OF BIRTH.

in my life who knew what the hell they were doing when it came to childbirth, so I hired her.

As it happens, even if I'd had a book-length list of birth preferences, it wouldn't have made a difference. I arrived at the hospital way too late for epidurals, Pitocin, any of the things women are supposed to have opinions about. Mollie dashed to the hospital when my husband called her—"Is this your sister?" asked my OB. "No, she's the doula," I replied. "Oh," she said, barely suppressing an eye roll, "the *doula*." Whatever.

Mollie was great throughout my delivery, though I didn't really leave her with much to do. I also, to my shame, cheated on her right to her face. The nurse by my right side, a slight African-American woman with purple eye shadow, somehow became my real doula. She gently rubbed my big toe and looked at me with such kindness and such confidence that I could do this, that I locked into her like she was an acid guide and I was in the freak-out tent at Woodstock. I would have followed her anywhere. John tells me I gazed at her throughout, adoration beaming out of my eyes. I really should have sent her some flowers.

2. I went to a birthing class. I'm not sure this counts, since it was just a one-day thing at the hospital I was scheduled to give birth at, not one of the weeks-long affairs held at places like the one where I found

my doula. It was run by a seen-it-all nurse in her fifties who showed us birthing videos that featured full, glorious thatches of pubic hair. There were a few other couples taking the class, including a South Asian couple who looked to be in their sixties and a couple from Staten Island, Tina and Carmine. The instructor started into a spiel about pain in childbirth and what partners could do to be helpful. "I mean, it's yoah fault," said Carmine. "Youse ate the apple." Later, Carmine went to the can; Tina looked helplessly at the group and said, "I swear, if we're only allowed one person in the delivery room, I'm gonna pick my mother."

The class's sole concession to woo-woo therapy-type stuff was an exercise in which each couple was to sit facing each other, knee to knee, and gaze into each other's eyes. We were supposed to tell each

CARMINE

other our deepest fears about childbirth and having a baby in general; I burst immediately into giggles that soon spiraled into uncontrollable laughter and was completely unable to get my shit together. The instructor looked amused at first, then annoyed, and finally alarmed as it became clear that I was having the laughing equivalent of a panic attack. I was sent out into the hallway to have some water and calm down, just like in elementary school.

A sweet coda to this story—as we were leaving the hospital, we saw the instructor in the lobby. "He seems nice in general," she said, jerking her chin at my husband, "but when he looks at you, the love in his eyes, lemme tell you." That was hands down the best piece of information I received that day.

3. I stared at a jar of fancy, expensive raw honey trying to remember if that was a thing I was supposed to eat or not.

4. I attended a pre-natal yoga class. Granted, this class was at the local Y, so it wasn't *that* fancy. I had never taken yoga before and have not taken it since. I am excruciatingly, mind-bogglingly bad at yoga. The instructor came over to put four (four!) blocks under my hands for

downward dog. "Is there . . . is everything all right?" she asked. Yeah, Moonbeam, I just have the tendons of a woman half my height and twice my age is all.

5. I asked for Aden & Anais swaddling cloths on my registry, received them, and cooed over them. I then failed to ever swaddle my baby properly in them, even once. She lived in hand-me-down fleece baby straitjackets until she was three months old.

6. Weekly mani-pedis and daily lymphatic massage. KIDDING!

7. I had pregnancy photos taken. Though in my defense, I wore a gorilla mask the whole time.

THIRD TRIMESTER:
THE DAMPENING

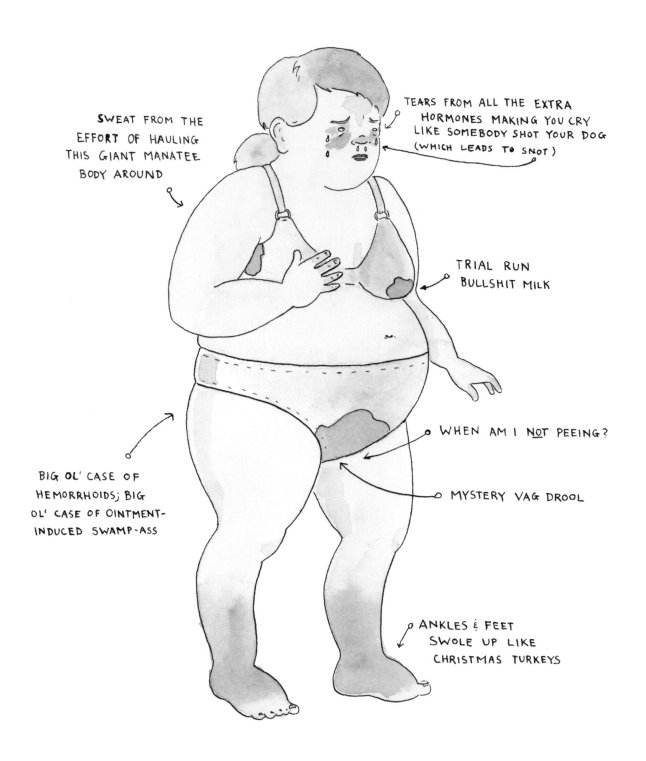

(OR: WHERE AM I LEAKING FROM TODAY?)

PREGNANCY CRAVINGS

OH, NOTHING MUCH...
IN PARTICULAR...

SAME SHIT I
ALWAYS WANTED,
I JUST GOT RID
OF ANY PRETENSE
OF SELF-
RESTRAINT

I'M CRAVING MEAT
IN THE WORST WAY.
RED MEAT.
RED, EXOTIC MEAT.
GIRAFFE.
RAW GIRAFFE.

I DUNNO,
AN ABORTION?

KIDDING!
KIDDING.

MOSTLY.

BABY SHOWER IDEAS

Baby Boot Camp

INVITATIONS: CONSCRIPTION FORM FROM THE U.S. GOVERNMENT

COLOR PALETTE: JUNGLE CAMO OR DESERT CAMO, DEPENDING ON THE SEASON AND WHICH WAR IS MOST INTERESTING TO THE LADY OF THE DAY

MENU: MRE'S, SHIT ON A SHINGLE, GOVERNMENT CHEESE

DECORATIONS: DECORATIONS ARE NOT REGULATION, SOLDIER

GAMES: SCALING WALLS WHILE CARRYING A RUCKSACK; COMMANDO-CRAWLING UNDER BARBED WIRE THROUGH A HAIL OF BULLETS—IF SHE CAN'T HACK THAT SHE'LL NEVER MAKE IT THROUGH LABOR

PARTY FAVORS: PURPLE HEARTS (CANDY, NATCH), SPENT BULLET CASINGS

I AM IN A WORLD OF SHIT—

Sorority Girls

INVITATIONS: NONE NEEDED. JUST HAVE THE PARTY COORDINATOR PUT ON A CLOAK AND HOOD AND SPIRIT THE ATTENDEES OUT OF THEIR BEDS

COLOR PALETTE: BITCH-PINK AND HOT BLACK

MENU: FOOD IS FOR FATTIES, FATTY

DECORATIONS: PAPIER-MÂCHÉ DICKS, DICKS MADE OF CARDBOARD, TINY PLASTIC DICKS

GAMES: STRIP PARTY GUESTS AND CIRCLE ALL FAT DEPOSITS WITH BLACK MARKER; MUSICAL CHAIRS BUKKAKE

PARTY FAVORS: HERPES

This Was Your Life

INVITATIONS: FUNERAL CARDS COMMEMORATING THE HONOREE'S LIFE AS A NON-MOTHER

COLOR PALETTE: SEPIA TONES

MENU: FOR NON-PREGNANT GUESTS: SMOKED DELI MEATS, RAW-MILK CHEESE, HARD LIQUOR, CIGARETTES FOR MOM: MUNG BEAN PASTE AND UNSALTED SALTINES

DECORATIONS: FLORAL WREATHS ARE ALWAYS A NICE TOUCH

GAMES: REMEMBER WHEN? REMINISCING ABOUT THE TIMES BEFORE THIS STUPID PREGNANCY HAPPENED

PARTY FAVORS: TINY GRAVESTONES ENGRAVED WITH THE WORD "FUN"

FUN

Rosemary's Baby

INVITATIONS: AN ANCIENT INVOCATION TO HASTUR WILL SUMMON ALL PARTY GUESTS

COLOR PALETTE: THE SALLOW LIGHT CAST BY A DYING SUN ON A WORLD LONG AGO DESTROYED BY AN ANGRY GOD

MENU: TRY THIS DELICIOUS NUTRITIONAL SHAKE!

DECORATIONS: GOATS, MOSTLY

GAMES: WHO'S YOUR DADDY? TRY TO GUESS WHETHER THE BABY'S FATHER IS HUMAN OR SUPERNATURAL IN ORIGIN

PARTY FAVORS: EVIL-MOJO BAGS, LASTING BOND WITH THE DARK LORD

NAMING THE BABY

My daughter's full name is Augustine Marlys Pastore. Her nickname is Tug, or Tuggie—I'm not entirely sure she even knows her real name. She might think "Augustine" is a thing I say when she's in trouble.

Deciding whether to give her my last name or her father's was a snap—who would intentionally saddle their kid with a last name like Flake? Middle was easy too; I wanted Marlys, after the little girl in Lynda Barry's hilarious, heartbreaking cartoons. I couldn't imagine a better role model than Marlys.

As for the first name, it was a process of elimination. I wrote down a list of fifty names, John ixnayed forty-eight of them. On that list were a few standbys—Catherine, Anne, Elizabeth—that were bumped because John had had girlfriends by those names. "Genevieve" was deemed "too Quebecois" by my ex-Montrealer husband. (Me: "What don't you like about *JEN-uh-veev*?" Him: "I just think *zhon-vee-EV*, and it's just such a [expletive for Francophone Canadians] name.") I liked Nola, after a great-aunt, but we both agreed it would seem like we named her after New Orleans—a great city, but we don't have any connection to it that would give us the right. The list was winnowed down to Augustine and Cecilia;

Cecilia was bumped when we (a) found we couldn't stop singing the Simon and Garfunkel song and (b) remembered that Cecelia was Jim and Pam on *The Office*'s baby's name.

And so: Augustine. The problem with Augustine was the nickname situation. I didn't want to name her Augustina for fear she would be a Tina, a name forever wedded in my mind to a friend of my mother's, a droopy, whiny sad sack of a woman with lank greasy hair and a sex-addict dog. "Gussie" and "Augie" sounded a little clunky, a little like spinster-aunt names from the forties, and not in a good way. But I had had "Tug" in my pocket for years, after reading a passage in *Portnoy's Complaint* where Alexander Portnoy sneeringly lists the nicknames of the friends of the high-toned shiksa he's fucking—*Poody and Pip and Pebble, Shrimp and Brute and Tug*—and while my own shiksa-ness lacks any pretense toward

WE ARE UNLIKELY TO FIND ONE OF THESE.

class, "Tug" jumped out at me. Adorable, I thought, and then didn't think about it again until I had a name in mind that needed a nickname and shared the letters "T," "U," and "G." This is what happens when dopes like me read books.

All this to say, her name is pretty random. But if there's one thing I can state with confidence, it's that no one in Brooklyn can give me any lip about giving my kid a weird name. Most of Tug's cohort have names that would have gotten their asses beat when I was a kid—Phineas, Freya, Declan. Auden, Zola, Dashiell. Bowie. *Denim*. Names that show up on a lot of "hipster baby name" lists, much to the chagrin of the parents. It's easy to laugh at some of these (I mean, *Denim*). It's a curious quality of creative-class types, hipsters, whatever you want to call them—this aversion to being the thing that they are. There's a Tumblr called Fuck Your Noguchi Coffee Table that mocks the chic, artsy decorating tastes that would lead one to, say, put antlers on the wall inside an empty picture frame, but getting the joke requires that you know what a Noguchi coffee table is in the first place. I'm no different; I chuckle mockingly at the characters on *Portlandia* and I absolutely own things with birds on them.

What you name your baby ultimately says something about *you*, and in a milieu where people are so uncomfortably self-conscious about what kind of people they are and are not, there're both a lot of names that are the equivalent of the artisanal pickle, class-signifier-wise, and a lot of anxiety about being artisanal-pickle-type people. Personally, I am weary of the conversation about what it means to be this or that sort of person. I *like* artisanal crap. It's *much nicer* than the crap that was around when I was a kid. I'm as guilty of eye-rolling as the next person, but seriously: name your kid Elik if that's your persuasion—as long as you have him vaccinated it's all fine with me.

Denim, though. Jesus.

SO. MUCH. STUFF.

The amount of crap you have—whether you need it, want it, or are obligated to haul it around on outings—is inversely proportional to the size of your child. Pregnant women and parents of newborns will find themselves awash in a sea of onesies, loveys, binkies, furniture designed to hold, feed, or sleep your child, and on and on and on. Your travel baggage situation explodes. Toddlers might not need a changing table or a high chair anymore, but their toy load gets out of control pretty quickly if not kept in check.

I am far from the first person to argue that perhaps we don't need all this crap. I am also a hypocrite—we have an awful lot of crap. Travel is basically the same as moving house at this point; between the car seat, the stroller, and the travel crib we're already looking at being in desperate need of a professional Sherpa. The smallest member of our family—the one who contributes nothing financially, and who cannot even be relied upon to wipe her own butt—*she* gets to travel with her own *furniture*. And she can't even *carry* it.

Of course in the early days, sometimes you have to sort through a lot of crap to figure out the crap that works. Our apartment is fairly good-sized by New York standards and a postage stamp anywhere else. And yet we managed to cram in several different iterations of a rocker-sleeper for Tug when she was small, a mix of hand-me-downs, shower gifts, and desperate Amazon purchases, until we figured out which one she would actually nap in instead of just flailing around looking distressed (one of these, an item which purported to possess soothing rocking powers, shuddered and buzzed like the world's smallest Magic Fingers bed). But everyone gets the emails from crap merchants who know you have, or are about to have, a child, and those people are going to try to sell you a wipe warmer. You do not need a wipe warmer. Nobody needs a fucking wipe warmer.

And don't give your baby too many toys. Keep a bucket or two in the living room or wherever they play and hide the rest. Rotate them out. Same as you do for a cat.

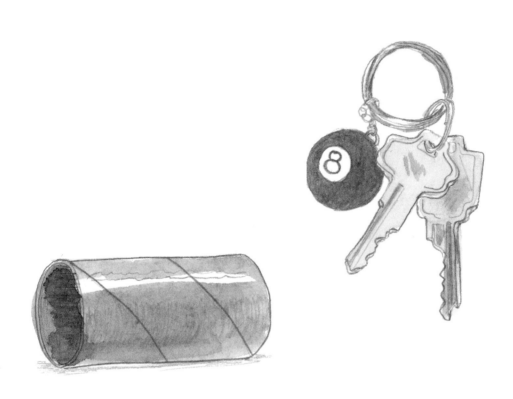

REALLY THE ONLY TOYS
YOU NEED FOR THE FIRST YEAR.

Baby Registries
of the 1%

Fetal Einstein
Your baby will be born speaking
Mandarin or your money back. Also available:
Quadratic Equations; Architecture; Finance

Prada Ring-Sling
Fits babies up to
55 lbs; mothers to
110 lbs. Comes in
black, grey, and
camel hair.

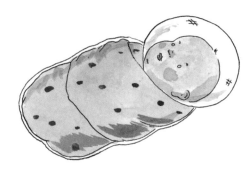

Germs-B-Gone Anti-Microbial Swaddle
Keep your baby calm and free
from the germs that are
everywhere, assailing him on all
fronts, unceasingly.

Enfamillions Flavored Formula

Don't let your child embarrass himself - and you - with his limited palate. Expand and refine his tastes with flavors like Brazilian Cacao, Foie Gras, and Stewed Ortolan.

Uppababy Urban Litter

Five-point harness keeps your little one safe while shoulder-height carry ensures superiority over all he surveys.

Loincloths, sandals sold separately.

HOME BIRTH:

Pros:

FLUORESCENTS REALLY ROB BIRTH OF ITS MYSTERY, DON'T YOU THINK?

LIGHT AT HOME MUCH MORE FLATTERING

I SPECIFICALLY REQUESTED A SIX-FOOT-BY-SIX-FOOT SACRED SPACE—

HOSPITALS FROWN ON BRINGING IN A SHAMAN

NO DOCS, NO DOCUMENTATION, AM I RIGHT?

EASIER TO KEEP THE BABY SECRET

HE STRAIGHT UP STARTED CRYING WHEN HE HELD HER, YOU BELIEVE THAT SHIT?*

*ACTUAL QUOTE!

NO NEED TO SHARE A RECOVERY ROOM WITH A SURLY TEENAGER

Cons:

FOR CHRIST'S SAKE, YOU'RE ONLY HAVING ONE KITTEN AND I DON'T THINK YOU EVEN PLAN TO EAT IT—

CAT WILL JUDGE YOU FOR DOING IT WRONG

AAAAAAAAAAANNNNN NNNNGGGGGGGGHHHHHH—

NEIGHBORS WILL HATE YOU FOREVER AND EVER

WHISKEY ≠ EPIDURAL

OK, OK, I SEE THE... OH, SHIT, THAT'S A HAND.

SOME SHIT LIKE THIS HAPPENS AND YOU HAVE TO BE MEDI-VAC'D TO DEB'S C-SECTION EMPORIUM 'N' GRILL

BIRTHING PLANS

PLAN A: AT HOME, ATTENDED BY MY PARTNER AND A TEAM OF SEX-POSITIVE DOULAS TRAINED IN HERBAL REMEDIES AND MASSAGE

PLAN B: AT A BIRTHING CENTER, ATTENDED BY A TRUSTED AND RESPECTED MIDWIFE

PLAN C: AT THE LOCAL HOSPITAL, ATTENDED BY WHOEVER HAPPENS TO BE ON DUTY

PLAN D: IN THE BATHROOM AT YOUR BEST FRIEND'S WEDDING, ATTENDED BY NINE GIN-AND-TONICS AND TOTALLY OUT OF THE BLUE

What Will You Do With Your Placenta?

HAVE IT DRIED, GROUND UP, AND
ENCAPSULATED TO TAKE IN PILL FORM

BURY IT UNDER A TREE WITH
THE REST OF THE EVIDENCE

LET YOUR CHILD KEEP IT AS A COMPANION

SOMETHING LIKE THIS, PROBABLY

HERE'S HOW IT WENT WHEN I HAD THE BABY

The day I got to thirty-seven weeks pregnant I woke up at 7 AM with "gas pains." You can see where this is going; I could not. I had stayed up late the night before watching *Sons of Anarchy* and trying to make a ridiculous curtain out of photo slides for the baby's room (don't ask). I'd experienced a bit of . . . leakage, but was passing that off as "bullshit my body is doing now because I pee every time I laugh." Thus the text I sent my doula (yeah, yeah) at 8:22: "Hey Mollie! Sploosh update: had a panty liner soaking incident last night and low belly pain this AM, but whether or not this is the real thing or just vag drool and a badly cornering crap is anyone's guess."

A tendency toward glibness can be a gift; it keeps you from panicking too quickly and can help leaven a heavy situation. It can also lead to you sitting on the toilet trying desperatcly to pass a stool that turns out not to be a stool at all. After an hour or so on the can, I called my doctor—I'm not a complete idiot—but only managed to connect with the clinic's answering service and a vague-sounding young woman who told me I should go to the ER, maybe, whatever. It was a pretty crappy clinic. I was convinced that were I to go to the hospital I would be met with scoffs and told to go home and fart on my own time, so I stayed in the bathroom, trying to poop, taking a bath, stroking the tiles very, very gently, and intermittently howling.

Around noon I became concerned that this "gas situation" might be hurting the baby, so I made an executive decision to call a car and go to the stupid hospital. Just like in the movies, I was in the back of a cab making little hoo-hoo-hoo sounds and trying to assure the driver I would not have a baby in his car, though I couldn't guarantee I wouldn't crap all over it. Luckily for everyone concerned, the hospital was only a mile away; when I got out of the cab I was holding my belly and bellowing like a sow. I was put in a wheelchair and whisked into an examination room, where I stroked the wall very, very gently and waited for a real doctor (they'd sent in a med student to take my family history; I was impolite to him). A real doctor showed up, took a look at my lady parts, and took out a walkie-talkie. "Clear a labor room," she said into it. "Wait, am I in labor??" I asked. "You," she said, clearly biting off the words "you idiot," "are having a baby RIGHT NOW." She said this because I was 9.5 centimeters dilated. That promise I made to the cabbie could very easily have been false, and I would have had the New Yorkiest of all possible birth stories to tell.

Only one thing saved the cab's upholstery: the baby was coming face-up. This is not nearly as worrisome as a butt- or feet-first baby,

THE FUCK JUST HAPPENED?

nor as awful as that thing where their head gets jammed to the side and they're somehow coming . . . neck-first? Yikes—but it does make the whole process a bit more difficult. There was an awful lot of pushing. I moaned piteously for ice.

It is perhaps worth mentioning here that I also had sort of a comedy bit prepared. In the labor scene of the imaginary movie I had been screening in my head for weeks, I had some great zingers, my favorite being something along the lines of "This is a hospital, right? Why don't you go find a surgeon and see if she can't figure out some way to make it physically possible to go fuck yourself?" Some ladies make playlists, some assemble sweet layettes; I, apparently, come up with needlessly vulgar insults to fling in the face of whoever is unfortunate enough to be on hand to bring my child into the world.

But: back to my face-up baby, stuck in the canal. After a couple of hours we had all had it with the pushing; I asked if maybe they didn't have one of those vacuum thingies handy? They did. Three contractions, a Hoovering, and a big doctor squeezing down on my belly later, out came the baby. The placenta was less eager to make its debut; the cord snapped, and my OB—a . . . *brisk* woman—reached on up there with her hand to pluck it out of me. She regarded it quizzically: "That's a really raggedy old-looking placenta," she said. I tried to think. Had I gotten my placenta from a thrift store? Am I that cheap? I couldn't remember. I took a look at it; it looked like Freddy Krueger in a bowl.

But raggedy old Freddy Krueger had done his job—the baby, while on the smallish side, was just fine, they said. She was fine, she was here in the world, and, much to my surprise, the world carried on like normal. Outside, it was still just a sunny, hot afternoon, Thursday just being a regular old Thursday, nothing different.

POST-PARTUM ACTIVITIES

SEE HOW BAD YOU CAN FREAK OUT YOUR
HUSBAND, BECAUSE YOU'RE A CRAZY LADY NOW

TAKE A POKE AROUND AND SEE WHAT
HISTORICAL DISASTERS YOUR LADY BITS REMIND YOU OF

FACEBOOKFACEBOOKFACEBOOKFACEBOOKFACEBOOKFACEBOOK

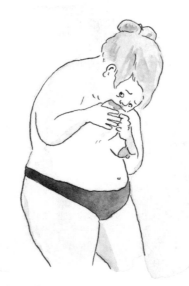

YOU'RE GONNA TRY THIS AT LEAST ONCE
SO YOU MAY AS WELL GET IT OVER WITH

POST-NATAL BIRTH CONTROL

CO-SLEEP UNTIL AGE 18

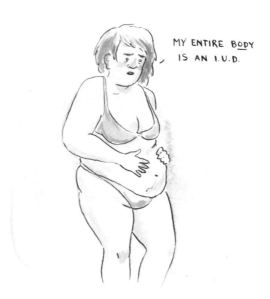

MY ENTIRE BODY IS AN I.U.D.

LET EXHAUSTION AND WEIGHT GAIN DO THEIR THING

ARE YOU SERIOUSLY NOT DONE YET?

QUICK, RESENTFUL HANDJOBS

IT ONLY FEELS LIKE CHEATING WHEN HE SPOONS HER.

IT.

WHICHEVER.

INVEST IN A REALDOLL™

POST-PARTUM SEX
(Are There Any Three More Erotic Words?)

Sex. Yeah. Wow. Remember when sex used to be some drunken inconsequential fun thing you did in the back of your car or in a basement or at the supply closet at work and then you had to go wash your hands after so you didn't go to a meeting smelling like balls? Hey, maybe one of those drunken inconsequential moments is even what put a baby in you!

But now there is a baby, and everything is different. Now one or more of your available holes is out of commission for the foreseeable future. Now you are both exhausted all the time. Now something squalls every five minutes so when are you supposed to find time to fool around? Now your body is fulfilling an entirely different function, and the thought of being functional in any other way makes you want to weep.

Here's an odd thing: I wanted to have sex again very soon after I had the baby. But not in a sexy way, not in a way that felt anything like sexual desire. What I felt was a physical jonesing for my husband's body that felt like starving. I would have cut him open and slept in him like a tauntaun if I could have. I did not want anything done to my lady parts; I was hardly at the point where I could bear to dab gently at them with toilet paper after taking one of my ginger, anxious pees. But I desperately, viscerally needed to be close to John. It was all tied up in hormones and weird post-partum loneliness and new, unpleasant feelings. It was not a particularly attractive look.

We spent the first couple of months of Tug's life on the fold-out bed in the living room, because it was bigger than our bed and lower to the ground, so I could get in and out of it more easily. Also, it was in the room where the TV lives, which was very important. Tug slept either in a nearby bassinette or with us in the bed. Here is where I have to pause and decide if I want Tug to know, sometime in the future when she can read, that her mother blew her father as she dozed in a little basket three feet away. She may not want to know that it was the least sexy, most inorganic coupling in her parents' history. All I felt was that psychotic craving for physical closeness. My come-on line was a classic: red-eyed, shaky with roiling emotions, I gestured to his area, and asked: "Do you mind if I see that for a minute?" TUG: THIS HAPPENED. GO WASH YOUR EYES OUT AND KNOW THAT YOU WILL NEVER AGAIN BE CLEAN.

It helped, a little, this act. It helped me feel a little closer to normal, even though this weird cannibalistic flesh-craving thing was all new and not super-awesome. I have never asked John how he felt about it. Men tend not to question the provenance or motivation behind hummers, even if the person dispensing them has spent most of the day crying.

"Normal," of course, is a term that shifts its meaning drastically over the course of one's life. "Normal" sexuality, for me personally, has meant a spectrum of things, from a Beautiful Expression of Love to ordinary belt-notching; it is unlikely to ever again mean "sport-fucking with an agreeable stranger." Some mourning goes along with the realization that your old normal is gone, no matter how ready you were to say good-bye to it. You have to mourn your old life, your dead selves, a little.

And your body, of course, is different. Luckily (maybe?) for me, I've never felt that my body was that great to begin with. I don't have to bemoan what childbearing did to my tits or my midsection; my tits have been lackluster since they first came on the scene and I have looked four months pregnant since I was eleven.

But your body is now a mom's body, which is a new thing to consider (and, I imagine, a harder thing to reconcile if your body didn't always look a little mom-ish). It changes your mental map of your physical land-scape. It gives a new dimension to how you consider your body. Maybe you now have a sense of awe at what your body is capable of, maybe you now have a sense of dismay at how it looks after being rearranged. When my boobs started producing milk I felt a surprised delight, kind of like if I'd suddenly discovered I could turn into a semi a la Transformers (I also felt relief, because colostrum doesn't make anybody feel like the whole breastfeeding thing is working out). I also felt keenly aware of my body as a fluid-producing machine. I didn't feel gross, exactly, I just felt very . . . damp. Swampy, fecund, cavewoman-like. My body, in other words, did not feel like a thing I would expect anybody to want to have sex with. Which is a weird thing no matter where you're at body-image-wise.

As of this writing my daughter is two; my nethers have recovered and my body, as opposed to the twenty-five percent more gross that it was for months after giving birth, is back to the regular-level gross it was before, more or less. My husband is contractually obligated to have sex with me and not with anyone else, and he fulfills those contractual obligations. It's better than it sounds.

The Early Days
(Welcome to Your New Home)

For the first four days of my daughter's life I was carried along by what I assume was a massive, and evolutionarily necessary, endorphin rush. I didn't really sleep, yet I felt giddy and relentlessly positive. My belly hung like a fleshy, deflating balloon and I couldn't move beyond a tentative amble, but I felt like this whole baby thing was totally copacetic, easy-peasy lemon-squeezy, no biggie—I got this, good times.

That feeling wore off.

What remained after the foam of adrenaline subsided was a raw, abraded, wounded creature. I felt like I had come out of a chrysalis too early. I felt like I had moved to a terrible new country where I didn't speak the language, and where the land might slide out from under me at any second. Nothing felt safe or right or familiar at all. It felt, oddly, like that fragile, abandoned feeling of having been dumped. I was crushingly lonely and also overwhelmed by having people around. I missed my husband desperately even though he was in the same room. A story, amusing in retrospect: our second day home, I was at the table working on an illustration; John was ten feet away, and I missed him so much I burst into tears all over my drawing. He was as alarmed as if I'd suddenly covered my head in tinfoil and started raving about Jesus. I cried like clockwork between the hours of 6 and 8 PM. I was convinced every time John left the house that he would be killed by a meteor or a drunk driver. The baby felt like a bomb that might go off at any minute. I wanted to scratch myself a hole in the ground to hide in. It was awful.

I was also terrified that those feelings would never end. Everything I looked at online said that post-partum awfulness lasted two weeks; at 2.5 weeks I started to panic. What if this was permanent? What if this was just how it felt to have a baby? I was half convinced that nothing would heal, from my brain to my heart to my nether regions, which I kept well sprayed with all the cooling analgesic spray I'd boosted from the hospital.

Except, miraculously, it did all start to heal. I don't remember an exact moment when the clouds started to break, but I know that after about three or four weeks I started to feel a little bit like I was coming around to myself. It was a slow process, but it built on itself. I'm very lucky that those shadows never lengthened into full-blown post-partum depression. On top of the whole Feeling Awful thing was the guilt I felt that I wasn't just over the moon and in love with the baby; drag that out over months and I do not know what I would have done (tried to get professional mental help, probably. That statement is a doorway into a whole other tirade about health care in America and mental health resources and *don't even get me started*). Depression is bad enough; depression plus baby? Fuck.

But what *were* my feelings toward my baby in those first few weeks? I have a hard time describing them as love, exactly. What I felt was more a combination of extreme fascination—I wanted to look at her, inspect her, hold her all the time—and profound duty. Maybe it was sort of an emotional colostrum, a pre-love. Which got me a little tangled up—what was wrong with me that I didn't feel that huge love-rush thing that people talk about? I kept waiting for it to happen, and messing myself up with fear that it wouldn't. But looking back now, I think what I felt toward her was more primitive and animalistic than what we think of as love, a deep need to protect and nurture and look at. Love, that messy, abstract, human thing—that came later. And it didn't come in some epic deluge of feeling—like everything else in this parenting deal, it knit itself together slowly, and without my volition. Like most things in life, it all got better when I got out of my own way.

THE FIRST TIME SHE SLEPT LONGER THAN THREE HOURS IN A ROW, I HALF-WOKE UP DURING HOUR FOUR THINKING "OH GOD, SHE'S DEAD." AND THEN THE NOT-AWAKE HALF WENT "WELL, IF SHE IS DEAD, WAKING UP NOW WON'T MAKE HER ANY LESS DEAD, SO JUST GO BACK TO SLEEP." AND THAT WOKE ME UP FOR REAL, BECAUSE HOLY SHIT I'M A

MONSTER.

THREE THINGS MY OB-GYN SAID AT MY SIX-WEEK FOLLOW-UP VISIT
(PLUS MY UNSAID RETORTS)

Let's Hit The Korova

My sister is, as I've mentioned, a post-partum nurse and a lactation consultant. Having somebody like this in the family when you're a new mother is a huge bonus—even if you pay to have such a person in your life, you can't reasonably expect them to answer your frantic 2 AM texts about proper latch technique (my sister also works the night shift, so she's usually up). The downside is that if you decide this exclusive breastfeeding thing is not working out, you're not just dismissing an employee—you're disappointing your family.

My daughter, while not technically premature, arrived early enough to exhibit some preemie-ish tendencies. Her sucking technique was lackluster, and she fell asleep on the boob after just a few minutes. In the hospital, they had me hand-express (so artisanal!) into a little cup, which my husband fed to her. "Guh!" he exclaimed as she swallowed—"I can feel it, like, moving down her back!" She was such a tiny, fragile thing. It's hard to imagine now.

In the first few days at home, I frantically tried to express into more little cups. I was distraught at how little there seemed to be—I knew this was the pre-milk stuff, but still, it seemed so scant. Tug was jaundiced;

she had to eat to de-yellow herself. Surely she wasn't getting enough from suckling halfheartedly for two seconds and then falling asleep. I poured my hand-expressed colostrum down her throat—you really *could* feel it going down, and it *was* weird.

A few weeks in, no longer yellow, and with a bit more meat on her bones, she needed more than thimble-sized shots of milk. She never got great at the latch, and I never got great at producing. I pumped while she napped, worrying the whole time that when she woke up, there'd be nothing left for her. I drank Guinness and ate lactation cookies. I took supplements that made me smell like maple syrup (which was an improvement over my bizarre, turbocharged post-partum B.O. Whether that can be chalked up to an extra-sensitive new-mama/not-smoking nose or there being some evolutionary reason to make new mothers stank beyond belief, I couldn't tell you). I never was able to pump more than four ounces of milk at a time, and Tug's hungry hours—from about 4 to 8 PM—were a shitshow. She would nurse, cry, nurse, get mad at my tits, cry, I would feed her my stashed milk, nurse her some more, rinse, repeat. All I thought about was milk and how to make more of it.

Then one night, as Tug flailed and wept at my breast, it came to me: FUCK THIS. They *made* something for this. I could solve both our problems with a quick trip to the pharmacy. But first, I called my sister.

"I think I'm gonna give her some formula," I said.

She was quiet for a minute.

SOMETHING I DOODLED WHILE ON THE
PHONE WITH THE PEDIATRICIAN

"Look," she said, finally, "I'm not gonna tell you you can't. But I will tell you it'll change her gut flora, her poop will be different, and you might start producing less. And formula smells disgusting."

"I will pour a forty out for Tug's poor dead gut flora," I replied. "This is driving us all insane."

The next day, I went and purchased my very first can of Enfamil. It sat on the counter, daring me to use it. You can never go back, it seemed to say to me. Once you open me up, your dream of exclusively breastfeeding is over.

Shut up, canister, I told it. That dream is making my daughter hungry and draining me—literally!—of all my strength. If dancing with the devil gets my daughter fed, so be it.

Tug got her first bottle of Corporate Non-milk that night. She horked it down so greedily it's like it was liquid heroin. She ate, she nestled in my arms, she dozed contentedly. It was amazing.

My sister was right—her poop did change, from that inoffensive corn-smelling stuff to something much more like actual human shit. It stopped her up for almost a week; I had to sodomize her gently with a lubed-up Q-tip to release the blockage. And yes, formula smells disgusting. But, as the saying goes—it filled a hole, and produced a turd.

In retrospect, it feels a bit silly to have gotten my panties so in a twist over the whole thing. But now that the societal pendulum has swung so far from the "science knows best!" heyday back toward breastfeeding, the pressure is very real. I see women all the time on Facebook and on Mothers' Group boards feeling like failures for not producing enough; strangers who see you mixing up a bottle in public will feel no shame about reminding you that "breast is best." Here's the thing: those are the same nosey Parkers that, thirty years ago, would have been aghast at you breastfeeding in public, and would have told you to put your baby on cow's milk at three months. People always feel entitled to say some shit to you about how you should be doing something differently. You are well within your rights to tell these people to go fuck themselves. How you get calories into your baby, whether you're casually whipping out a tit in public or mixing formula with water from a public drinking fountain, is nobody's goddamn business but your own. Breast is great, I'll give it that. The nutritional profile is great. Free milk is great. But best? What's best is having a happy, fed baby, and minding your own beeswax.

HOW TO TIE A SWADDLE

THE PAID PROFESSIONAL

THE MACGYVER SPECIAL

THE ELEGANT SOLUTION

THE LONG SLEEP

THE DOWNSIDES of PUMPING

LACKLUSTER PRODUCTION CAN LEAD TO A WHOLE NEW KIND OF BODY DYSMORPHIA

SOMETIMES YOU FORGET IT'S NOT COOL TO ANSWER YOUR DOOR LIKE THIS

ONCE YOU START TO HEAR WORDS IN YOUR PUMP'S NOISE, YOU WILL NEVER BE ABLE TO STOP HEARING THEM

DANGER OF DEVELOPING MATERNAL FEELINGS FOR YOUR "ELECTRONIC BABY"

BREAST FEEDING F.A.Q.'s

Breast milk is nature's perfect food for your baby, and breastfeeding creates a strong and lasting bond with your child. However, as with any undertaking, there are bound to be some bumps along the way. We here at LactaMama have compiled a list of some of the most common breastfeeding issues and offer advice from our team of lactation experts.

MY BABY FALLS ASLEEP AT THE BREAST.

"Lazy baby" syndrome is common, but it's important to remember that breastfeeding is a calming, soothing activity for your child. If being at the breast lulls your child to sleep, try to make breastfeeding a bit more interesting for your child. Sing to her in a loud voice, or clear your throat several times in a row. Nurse in

noisy public places, like the subway or construction sites. Stimulate her by tickling her feet or pricking him slightly with a pin. Consider painting one or both of your breasts a bright neon shade.

MY BABY CAN'T LATCH ON PROPERLY.

If you've introduced nipple substitutes such as a bottle or a pacifier into your baby's mouth, you may have damaged her ability to latch on to your breast. Immediately stop using all false nipples. Have your baby checked

CORRECT.

NEEDS
CORRECTION.

for tongue-tied or other oral deformities, which may require surgery. An entire reshaping of the oral cavity may be needed, or a surgical reshaping of your nipple to accommodate your baby's mouth style.

BABY SPITS UP AFTER BREASTFEEDING.

Take a look at your diet—there is likely something in there that upsets your baby's delicate tummy. Eliminate dairy, wheat, eggs, sugar, soy, corn, berries, seeds, and nuts. (A nutritional paste free of all

these irritants is available at LactaMamaShop.com.) After a month you may reintroduce these things one at a time, but be sure to wait two weeks between each introduction.

I'M NOT PRODUCING ENOUGH MILK.

Consider a Nursing Sequester—spend three weeks in a darkened room with your baby and nurse round-the-clock. Have your partner bring you your three daily servings of LactaMama nutritional paste. As you eat, remind your body that you are taking in nourishment to provide nourishment

using the "food in, food out" mantra. Make sure the room is free of all distraction such as television, Internet, or radio. Keep conversations with your partner to a minimum—this is baby's time.

I'M PRODUCING TOO MUCH MILK.

There is no such thing. Surplus milk can be made into cheese and yogurt for when your little one is ready for solids. A strong producer can keep her

children in mama-made dairy products until college.

BABY FUSSES AT THE BREAST.

Fussing usually occurs when something about the mother is upsetting the baby. Eliminate all perfumes and fabrics other than pure cotton, linen, or silk. Modulate your speaking voice to a pleasant, low tone. Control your thoughts so that no negative emotions adversely affect your flavor profile. Choose a focus object—preferably something cheery, like a special rock, and if unhappy thoughts intrude, focus on your object and banish them. Remember that thought is a voluntary process, so the choices you make here are crucial to your child's health and well-being. If your partner is engaging in negative thinking, make sure he or she is out of the room while this important bonding experience takes place.

EASY-TO-MAKE TINFOIL CHAPEAU

NIPPLES CRACKED/BLEEDING.

It's important to remember that blood does not have nearly the nutritional value of breast milk. If your nipples are bleeding, your child may not be getting enough

SYMPTOM OF NIPPLE FAILURE

milk—so make sure you nurse for extra-long sessions. An improper latch is usually the cause of nipple failure (see above re: correcting your baby's latch).

CAN I BREASTFEED IN PUBLIC?

Breastfeeding in public is not just your right, it's your duty. As a breastfeeding ambassador, you have a unique opportunity to educate the public about the benefits of breastfeeding. No need to hide behind a nursing cover—let your bare breast be a testament to your dedication to natural, Goddess-given nutrition.

♥"SLEEP"♥

I love to sleep. One of my favorite things as a child was to wake up on a Saturday morning and, freed from the sorrowful task of getting ready for school, hover deliciously in the twilight space between wakefulness and sleep, drifting back into Slumberland as many times as I liked. As I grew up I became a dedicated night owl—I remember the summer I was fourteen, just before I was old enough to find a job, regularly staying up until sunrise, listening to R.E.M.'s *Reckoning* on cassette over and over again, drawing, reading, and generally farting around until I passed out, and waking up in the midafternoon. Waking is a slow and torturous process for me, with lots of disoriented stumbling and painful, heavy limbs, trying to find my way out of the thick, dislocating fog and make something of my day, goddammit. For this reason, I've never been a good napper. Instead of revitalizing me, naps put me right back into the deep water, and fighting my way back to full consciousness is a battle I really only want to wage once a day.

All this to say: I was ill suited for the sleep deprivation part of new motherhood.

Concepts like "day" and "night" disappeared. Tug would sleep for an hour, or two, maybe three, wake up, cry, muddle around on my tit, get a new diaper, blink for a while, fall back asleep, and repeat. "Sleep when the baby sleeps," people would tell me, and then I would consider punching them in the face. This cycle mode meant I was always struggling up out of the deep water, trying to wake up. I was also never fully asleep, because evolutionary remnants deep in my brain were keeping me hyperalert in case of saber-toothed tigers. Hurricane Sandy hit when Tug was four weeks old; my biggest fear was that we would lose Netflix. I watched the entire series of *Trailer Park Boys* and cried when I ran out of episodes. I watched *The Accused* with the sound off. I watched *Angel Heart* with the sound on and figured Mickey Rourke and Lisa Bonet fucking in a rain of blood probably just looked like blobs of light to her anyway.

About three weeks in, John and I returned home from a walk (an amble, really). I sat my tattered ass down on the fold-out bed and turned on the TV. John looked at me, leaning closer in concern. "Your face is *gray*," he said. "I feel weird," I said. "Why don't you go lie down in the bedroom for a while and I'll watch the Netflix? And the baby?" he said. "That sounds okay." I stumbled into the bedroom. I hadn't actually lain down in the marital bed since returning from the hospital. It felt odd. I tried to sleep, but adrenaline and saber-toothed-tiger–fighting hormones were making it difficult. I fucked around on my phone for a while. I got tense about how much potential sleep time I was wasting fucking around on my phone. I finally fell asleep. Around midnight John came into the room. "I'm so sorry," he said. "She's crying and we're out of pumped milk." I

gulped a few mouthfuls of air and tried to surface. I'd been asleep for four hours, which should have felt luxurious, and instead felt like whatever it is they do in torture scenarios where they show you a little mercy *just to soften you up* and then carry right on torturing you again. I shuffled back to the NetflixDrome and got my tits out.

I wish I could tell you there was some magical solution to all of this that we hit on. There wasn't; it's just a thing you have to go through with newborns. Her sleeps started to coalesce a bit after a couple of months, and got better when we finally folded up the infernal sofa bed and put her in her own room. They didn't coalesce automatically into a hefty eleven-to-twelve-hour block, however, which was a situation I longed for desperately. And thus, we come to sleep training.

I suspect that "sleep training" might outrank certain porn genres in terms of Google searches. I mean, not the heavy hitters like "girl-on-girl" or "barely legal teens," but I bet "sleep training" beats, say, "devil's three-way" or "shit on a glass table." Definitely more hits than "lusty secretary 60+" or "gay bear scheisse films." This is because nothing is more important than sleep. Nothing. Maybe water. But like most very essential things, you really don't notice how much you need it until suddenly, disastrously, you don't have it anymore.

At some point, your child will have to be taught how to sleep by himself. Unless you're Family Bed people. If that's your jam, have at it, hippies. Sleep training is a crucial theater in the Mommy Wars—people just go batshit insane on the subject. Reading the comments to anything ever is a bad idea, but take a look at how people go at each other's throats sometime in any online discussion of sleep training. "Cry-it-out is cruel and barbaric!" "Co-sleeping will make your kid a clingy, dependent mess!" "You're a terrible mother! Somebody should call DCYS!" "MYOB, you fucking cunt!" Things escalate quickly when you're sleep deprived.

Sleep training also provides publishers a great opportunity to sell you books. You will buy a bunch of them, because you are insane with exhaustion. They will all tell you different things. You read them because you desperately want to be told how to get out of this sleep-hole you're in. You get confused. You cry.

Again, I don't have a lot to offer in terms of tips or actual sleep-training advice. I will tell you that what appealed to me was any philosophy that could be summed up in three sentences and didn't involve some elaborate song and dance and carefully timed intervals and yadda yadda yadda. Our pediatrician recommended a three-day CIO regimen of putting her down and not reentering the room until morning; we never ended up going that hard-core, but we did get good at distinguishing the "I'm pissed that you guys put me in here, you better come get me you assholes" cry from the "Help help I'm on fire and/or have shit my pants" cry and ignored or assisted accordingly. She dropped her last wee-hours feeding around eight months, but I honestly don't remember if that was my idea or hers. I, however, still find myself up at odd hours watching *Trailer Park Boys*.

Mommies' Groups

Before I got pregnant, the idea of a Mothers' Group—or the more-worryingly styled "Mommies' Group"—made me shudder. What could be more boring, more of a complete abnegation of your old, awesome self, more of an icky Mommy Culture nightmare than sitting in a room with a bunch of other stupid babies and their stupid moms?

And then I had a baby.*

Baby care, especially in the early days, is lonesome, isolating work. You have, in effect, moved to a new country, one where you don't know anyone yet and you haven't moved any of your stuff in and your friends won't come visit you because you live on the moon and if they do, all of a sudden you don't speak the same language anymore. And you're tired and insane and your tits hurt and your taint is ruined and you miss your partner even though they're right here because all of a sudden Everything

---

* "And then I had a baby" is a phrase I say about twelve times a day, usually in reference to something about which I have had to revise my opinion, something I said I would never do that I totally do all the time, or one of the legion of things about which I have turned out to be dead wrong.

Is Different and you don't know who anyone is anymore. This is when that stupid room of stupid babies starts looking pretty good.

Someone in my neighborhood had the brilliant idea to open a coffee shop with a little attached room outfitted with a padded floor and toys. The Internet informed me that this was a place where a New Moms group met on Fridays. I am glad I live here, in the future, where the Internet and baby cafes exist, because I quite possibly would have lost my goddamn mind if I had not met those other moms. Your other friends—your friends from your old country, where you lived before you had a baby—will eventually* get sick of you talking about latch problems and newborn shit patterns. In a Mothers' Group, you get to drill right on down on that business. You will learn more about other people's bodily functions than you ever thought you wanted to know. My group came complete with a message board, giving me the option of posting insane-person questions at 3 AM and, more often than not, getting a response.

An unexpected side benefit to all this is that I met some ladies—and men!—that I would have wanted to befriend even if we didn't have children the same age. Some of this can be chalked up to my being lucky enough to live in a neighborhood that's pretty much asshole-to-elbow with babies at the moment and filled with more-or-less like-minded folks; I did not have

---

* quickly.

to go especially far out of my comfort zone to make these new friends. But that said, babies are the great leveler: politics, socioeconomics, whether or not you're into drum'n'bass—all of these things are irrelevant in the face of extreme sleep deprivation.

You will get more comfortable in your new country. It takes time, is all. But there's wisdom in the way immigrants huddle around each other for comfort in the New World, building communities and finding their feet before venturing out into the suburbs and forgetting they ever liked pierogi: joining up with other newcomers is immensely helpful and tremendously comforting.

It's also not quite so easy as that. Making new friends as an adult is weird. By the time we're in our baby-having years most of us have gelled, if not calcified, in terms of the kind of things we like to do and who we like to hang around with; one of the big ways having a baby can change up your sense of identity is that it changes things as fundamental as how you spend your day and with whom you spend it. There's a lot of awkwardness involved in feeling out other parents on the playground or in the coffee shop, and when you meet one you like, there is the even-more-awkwardness of figuring out how to woo them into being your friend. It's a process most of us haven't had to go through since high school or college, and this time, we don't get to get shit-faced drunk to facilitate it.*

But even if you're shy, or awkward, or prone to making vulgar, entirely inappropriate jokes (and I have been all of these things at times), there is a group for you. Even if that group is just one other mom who you caught rolling her eyes at a diaper cake or a bunch of ladies you've never met on Facebook. Community: it's not just for hippies!

---

*   not entirely true.

MY BEST FRIEND vs. MY BREST FRIEND™

MY BEST FRIEND...

Stays up late into the night with me, drinking whiskey and talking about ridiculous things.

Lets me bum cigarettes.

Knows what I was like at 19.

Has a pet name for me.

Has this running gag with me where we make lists for each other on our birthdays of reasons why we love each other, which started off as a cruel satire of a sweet-but-too-sweet letter I got from a boyfriend.

Gave a speech at my wedding.

Is great on road trips.

MY BREST FRIEND™

Is a body-hugging pillow with a belt, sheathed in terrycloth.

Is covered in milk and spit-up.

Is a sickly shade of mint green (where not discolored by milk or vomit).

Smells awful, but I can't seem to get it together enough to wash it.

Is often shunted aside for the other, cleaner pillow, which keeps slipping away because it needs a belt, at which point I curse and retrieve the Brest Friend.

★ SEPTEMBER SHOWS AT THE A-WEENA ★
A ROCK PERFORMANCE PLAY SPACE

Hi Parents! We've got a sweet September coming up here at the A-Weena- loads of great bands for tots and parents (and caregivers!) to rock out to!

Sept. 1st: Back to Skool with Fanny and the Eraserheads! Get ready to hit those books to Fanny's educational classics like "One, Two, Three and Me" and "Me Tarzan, Euclid." Math-rock at its best! Noon-1PM

Sept. 4th: The Dan Zanies: A Dan Zanes Tribute Band. Hear your favorite hits from the former Del Fuego Dan Zanes, as interpreted by the guys from the Summer '12 Dads' Group! 3-4PM

Sept. 7th: Velvet Playground featuring "Grandma Mo" Tucker. Free drum clinic for kids 5 and up! 2-3PM

Sept. 10th: Barney and Friends Tuvan Throat Singing. You've heard "I Love You, You Love Me," but you've never heard it quite like this! 1-2 PM

Sept. 13th and 27th: House Band AC/WeeC takes the stage! Free juice and cookies for kids, free grown-up shots for Mom and Dad (one per customer, please). 10 AM - until the juice runs out

Sept. 20th: TRENCHMOUTH (Chicago), SHADES APART (NJ) opens. Doors at 5:30. All ages. Free juice.

Sept. 25th: Who's got Daddy's Balls? All-day punk festival. The Dependents (kid-friendly Descendents covers) headline. 10-6. $50.00 for an all-day wristband.

Every Wednesday is Nanny Day with the Irie Three! Reggae, soca, rocksteady, and dub hits from the islands. Something special for your child's favorite person. Noon.

Remember, our Soft Room is here for you every day from 9AM-7PM. Padded floors for the little ones, padded walls for you!

Rock On!

♥, Team A-Weena

Avondale Heights Moms BURN BOOK!

Lauren K. thinks BF-ing is gonna cancel out all the cookies she eats at the meet-ups = NOPE!

Sarah M's son Jayson is a spoiled rotten little shit and I'm totally gonna let my son beat the crap out of him.

PATTY F'S BABY IS FUUUGLY

EVERYONE WANTS TO FUCK YOUR HUSBAND ADELITA

FOR FUCK'S SAKE RACHEL WHEN YOU'RE DONE NURSING PUT YOUR TITS AWAY

DIVORCE BETTING LINE

Tara + Jim: 3:1
Marilyn + Steve: 4:1
Lauren P. + Chris: 6:1
Leanne + Samantha: 2:1
Susan + Jake: 1:1

↑

SUSAN + JAKE FTW BECAUSE I SAW JAKE HITTING ON SOME 20 Y/O AND PLUS SUSAN'S A BITCH

CAROL SEZ CHARLIE HAS ECZEMA BUT I KNOW RINGWORM WHEN I SEE IT

Nobody cares what your therapist says, Jill.

OMG BETH SHUT UP ABOUT YOUR KID'S ALLERGIES OR ELSE I'M GONNA PUT A PEANUT UP HIS ASS

VANESSA— GET THAT GODDAMN CRADLE CAP UNDER CONTROL YOU ARE GROSSING US ALL OUT

John Is A Daddy

Deep in my sketchbook from my first year in art school there's a page of dads. I'd taken my then-six-year-old nephew to a playground and was occupying myself drawing the fathers watching their children. Accompanying the drawings is some typical nineteen-year-old pseudointellectual bullshit: "This is how the daddies stand. It's their belts that bisect them and negate their sexuality. When men reach a certain age, they begin to be defined by their clothes in a different way—they convey 'daddy' instead of 'male'—in this they become more like women, existing for another's purpose instead of their own.* Responsible. Kindly. Benevolent. Scary. Scary because of the potential of *betrayal* of the fatherly pose—no man is *just* a father."

Buried in the ridiculous Lofty Thoughts verbiage, there's an idea that's worth reexamining now that I'm almost twice the age I was then and have become a parent myself. Whereas in some societies fatherhood is associated with manliness and virility (particularly if you've been lucky

---

* Paglia much? Jeeeesus.

enough to produce boys), in ours it sometimes seems to correlate with a softening, with being defanged and domesticated. Maybe that's because in our society we've begun to ask men to pull their weight in the child-rearing sphere instead of just planting those children in women's bodies and then swaggering off to smoke a cigar and compare dick sizes.

Happily for me, John has never been one for belted khakis (and especially given the style of pleat-front pants that plagued society in 1996, I stand by my assessment of them as sexiness-killers). But one of the most unexpected pleasures of parenting has been watching him become not a father, but a *daddy*. It is truly the loveliest thing. I had the feeling when I learned Tug's gender that she would be a daddy's girl; I certainly was. What I did not expect was, especially as she began to grow and become more of a person, how much *he* would belong to *her*.

He, of course, has some ineptitudes that are as funny as they are cli-chéd. If he dresses her, she looks homeless. He hasn't the faintest idea how to make a pigtail. As I write this, it occurs to me that he has never given her a bath (we're going to have to have a talk about that later). He is not shaping up to be much of a disciplinarian. I suspect he is poorly equipped to withstand the onslaught of big sad-eyes and pouty-lip that are endemic to raising a girl. But the *delight* this man takes in his child—it is truly something to see. Some of my favorite texts have been when I've been out and he's been in charge: "Not much to report here except that TUGJUSTCRAWLEDACROSSTHEFLOOR!!!""Himommy,Ijustpulledmyselfto a standing position by myself and stood there alone for over a minute NO BIGGIE." She Tigger-jumps on his belly and builds Lego towers with him and curls up next to him to watch Dora, and it is wonderful. As it happens, one of my two best friends had a son a year after Tug was born; watching him become a father has also been a rare and unexpected joy. In fact, fatherhood looks good on pretty much all of my guy friends who have taken the plunge.

What would I say to nineteen-year-old me, if I could go back in time? Besides a general ass-kicking and a stern admonishment to not blow the whole next semester and maybe don't sleep with *every* person that offers? I'd tell her this: that when she sees her man become a father, it won't look a thing like this neutered, suburban vision of anodyne daddyhood she's imagining. That the joy of watching the love between father and child will take her breath away sometimes. That it will be an experience richer and more precious than anything she's ever experienced before. And then we will talk about how awful, how fucking god-awful, pleat-front khakis are.

BABY CARRIER OPTIONS

IT LEAVES MY HANDS FREE TO WORK ON MY JEWELRY.*

* ROLL A DOOB.

THE SLING

IT'S VAGUELY LESS EMASCULATING THAN A STROLLER.

THE "BACKPACK" STYLE

YOUR MOTHER, SHE IS WHORE.

THE UNDERPAID IMMIGRANT

IT'S A CARDBJÖRN! GEDDIT??

THEY'RE GONNA LOVE THAT JOKE IN PRISON.

THE CARDBOARD 'N' PACKING TAPE D.I.Y. SPECIAL

STROLLER ACCESSORIES

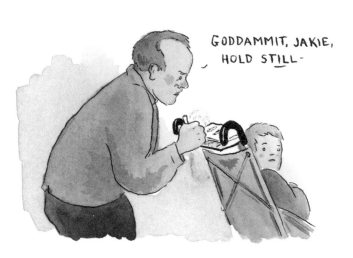

PARENTS' CONSOLE WITH COKE MIRROR

NOISE-CANCELLING HEADPHONES

TRUCK NUTZ FOR STROLLERZ!

CUPHOLDERS; CREEPING SENSE OF DISLOCATION OVER GETTING SO JAZZED UP OVER A CUPHOLDER

Dear Teeth,

Fuck you. Fuck you right in your enamel-coated, pulp-filled little fuck-hole. Fuck you for tearing your way through my baby's gums. I know she needs you. You know she needs you. You know who doesn't know that? THE BABY. All she knows is that everything used to be cool, mouth-wise, but now her food-hole is a screaming pain-hole of misery. Who did the engineering here? Couldn't you have formed up along with the rest of her? It's not like we have to wait for her *bones* to come in (though, boneless baby— hilarious! And delicious!). It's not like one day her *ears* erupted from her head in a torrent of blood and wails. Nope, just you. You're the toothy-come-lately that Ruins Everything. We had her nights *down*, do you understand how important that is? She was a sleep *champion*. Twelve hours at a stretch! I was finally catching up on *Game of Thrones!* My husband and I were able to engage in actual sexual intercourse with a reasonable expectation of being able to finish! We got *whole nights of sleep!* And now,

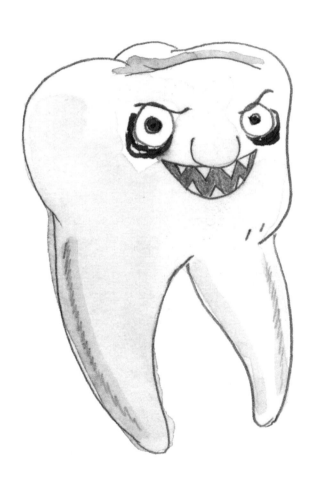

you've come, and we're right back in the newborn days, except worse, because now she can bite me.

She has five of you little fuckers now. Five brutal, frantic trials-by-fire down. How many to go? How many teeth do kids have? Twenty? Forty? Eleventy-four? Either way, I sure wish we'd bought stock in ibuprofen because she's chugging that shit like it's cheap yellow beer and she's a college freshman with something to prove. We even bought her one of those stupid amber necklaces but it didn't do a damn thing except make us look like hippie-dippy easy marks and pose a strangulation hazard. And let's face it, kids are clumsy as shit—she's only gonna knock half of you out by the time she's five anyway. Which I guess is why you get a mulligan on the first set of teeth, but still. This whole system, it's fucked up and bullshit. If they can come up with a drug that suppresses the first set of teeth and comes with a set of baby dentures, you can bet I'll be first in line. Because I need some goddamn sleep, Teeth, I really, really do. But in the meantime, fuck you, fuck you, fuck you.

Love,

Mama and Daddy

Why is my baby crying?

JUST REALIZED HE'S NEVER
GOING BACK TO THE WARM BAG
OF WATER HE USED TO LIVE IN

CANNOT BELIEVE HE'S STUCK
WITH YOU AS A PARENT

IS FULL OF BROKEN GLASS, APPARENTLY

FUCKING WITH YOU

WHAT'S THAT RASH?

BEDBUGS

ALLERGIC TO AIR

FAILURE BUMPS

A WART? OR TREE-MAN DISEASE??
OH SHIT OH SHIT IT'S TREE-MAN DISEASE

HOUSE CLEANING

My apartment is never cleaner than when I have a deadline. Generally speaking, the more apprehensive I am about a project, the more likely I am to find myself unable to work on it until I GET THOSE GODDAMN CLUMPS OF CAT HAIR OUT OF THE CORNERS, WHAT ARE WE, SAVAGES? Mind you, I am neither a clean nor a tidy person by nature. My husband is; that he stuck around after seeing the hoarder-hole horror of my bedroom the first time leads me to conclude that I must be very, *very* good at sex. But I am not a semiferal twentysomething anymore. I *like* to clean—it gives me a clear, simple sense of accomplishment, and the rewards are immediate.

That said, I don't really know much of anything about *how* to clean. In a recent paroxysm of self-loathing brought on by the realization that I had to ask Google every time I wanted to know how get burnt shit off a pan, I turned to Amazon and bought a Martha Stewart homekeeping encyclopedia and a whole mess of cleaning instruments.

Of course, what I really wanted to buy was *competence* (and if Amazon ever figures out a way to sell that I will stop bitching about how they're ruining it for the mom-and-pops and just go ahead and declare them the

One True Store). I frequently find myself in situations where I am staggered by my general lack of basic adult competence, housekeeping or otherwise. It's like that dream where you show up at school even though you're in your thirties and you've been skipping first and second period all year and do you even know your schedule?? Isn't it halfway through the semester?? Like that, only in real life and not about school.

But back to the cleaning issue: My husband is a tidier, but not a cleaner, per se. Our arguments almost always center around the state of our apartment. It usually begins with an exasperated request that I please, please, for Christ's sake, beat back some of the piles of crap on the dining table. Because I am an eight-year-old, I always counter with something about how I always scrub the tub and HE NEVER SCRUBS THE TUB. Accusations are batted back and forth until I agree to manage my crap piles, he acknowledges that I do all the dishes, and we both retreat to our respective corners to count dust bunnies and smolder.

As much as I like to use housekeeping as a procrastination device, inevitably I find myself in the weeds with work and

look up to find that the place is hazmat-level disgusting. Stickiness is a feature of life with a toddler; if not rigorously managed, it quickly gets out of control. Add cat hair into that mix and you have yourself a woeful situation.

I am certain there are good ways to deal with this. Ways involving chore wheels and cleaning schedules. I personally only know three: ignore it, hire somebody, or go on a late-night cleaning binge. I am an expert at the first, but even *my* patience for it runs out when confronted with the sight of my daughter sitting in a bath full of floating clumps of hair. The late-night cleaning has its advantages, not least of which is that I'm certain it annoys our horrible downstairs neighbor (I am careful not to clean the part of the apartment that is over our other, much nicer neighbor). But when you really need it done right, there is just no substitute for professional help. This is not an option for all of us, and it is only sometimes an option for me, depending on how work is going. I also feel extremely weird about having somebody else do my chores. But recently, I have been able to have a lady come and clean once a month and oh my God, it is so CLEAN afterward—it's unlike anything I've ever been able to accomplish, even with the Martha Book by my side. I can't buy competence, but I can rent somebody else's. This month, anyway.

She doesn't do crap piles, though. I will have to ask Amazon what I should do about those.

STAIN GUIDE

WHAT'S THE STAIN? ↓	WHAT'S IT ON? → ONESIE	BLANKIE	STUFFED ANIMAL	"NICE" OUTFIT
SHIT	Wrap onesie in paper and place in garbage	oxi-clean and a blind eye	Baby's first pet funeral	Why the fuck are we bothering putting babies in nice outfits? They don't care and they hate buttons. Don't put expensive clothes on somebody who shits and pukes professionally is the takeaway here.
MILK/ FORMULA	Whatever, it just blends right in	Let it set; wonder why baby smells like old cheese	Use animal in ritual sacrifice	
VOMIT	Oh, that's just milk that's been inside the baby	Wash out with tears	Trim dried vomit out of fur; use as way to explain mange	
BLOOD	cold water and self-recrimination	Bring to forensic lab	Play aminal hoppital	
FUCK IF I KNOW	Eh, who cares	Whatever	Fuck it	

PREPARING YOUR HOME FOR TODDLERS

KITCHEN:

- Put wine in a place inaccessible to children and easily accessible to you.

- Have "DON'T DO IT" and "THINGS WILL GET BETTER" engraved on all cutting implements.

- Make sure freezer is well stocked with emergency items like cake and cigarettes.

- Put your cleaning supplies somewhere where you can't hear them laughing at you.

- Keep a drawer full of menus of places that deliver quickly and feature things your toddler will actually eat

BATHROOM:

- Cover all your mirrors and burn all your scales

- Install a lock and chain on the door to ensure uninterrupted "Mommy Time."

- Replace current shower head with one better suited to furtive sexual gratification.

- Remove all special, expensive personal care products and put them somewhere where the baby won't knock them over and spill them all over the goddamn place

COMMON AREAS:

- Invest in a separate Netflix account so your partner is unable to see your soft-core viewing habits.

- Put all fragile knick-knacks in a glass-front cabinet, and make sure your child is aware that said cabinet is haunted.

- Establish a "toy prison" for toys- usually given by well-meaning grandparents-that light up, make loud sounds, or speak. Furlough these items only for the duration of a visit from the toy's giver.

- Outfit your child in a suit of bubble wrap to obviate the need for ugly "corner bumpers" on your furniture.

WHO'S DOING MORE?

Sick of being the one who empties out the diaper pail? Your partner always on your case about it being your turn to do bath time? Save your relationship—and your sanity—with this handy rewards system!

POINTS VALUES

Bath: 2 points

Diaper change: 2 points

Feeding: 3 points

Bottle/pump washing: 5 points

Nighttime feeding: 10 points

Blown-out diaper: 15 points

Blown-out diaper that involves baby's hair: 25 points

Blown-out diaper that involves your hair: 100 points

Vomit: 40 points

POINTS VALUE *(continued)*

Tantrum lasting longer than 5 minutes: 50 points

Cleaning the high chair: 15 points

Cleaning the stroller: 20 points

Actually lifting up the car seat pad and Hoovering out the Cheddar Bunny/juice slurry: 100 points

Weekend with in-laws: 100 points to spouse; 50 extra points for keeping cool during inevitable discussion of politics

POINTS REDEMPTION

+50 points: 2 hours of "alone time" to be spent according to your wishes

+100 points: "Girls' [or Boys'] night out," not to exceed 5 hours in length

+500 points: Partner must perform sex act of your choosing (naps count as sex acts)

+1000 points: Partner must care for child while you are hungover, and not disturb you or hassle you in any way, and may not scold you for drinking too much, because for Christ's sake, can you not just let your hair down every once in a while? Jesus!

+5000 points: Partner must take child on overnight trip, during which time you may hire a sex worker and/or housekeeper

Imbalances in excess of 10,000 points are grounds for divorce in NY, NJ, CT, WY, AK, and CA

WHO'S RAISING MY BABY?

My husband and I both work from home, which makes us luckier than just about anybody. But the key word in there is "work"—so while we are technically home, it is still necessary for us to outsource a certain amount of our child care so we can actually get that work done.

I am a freelancer and my husband runs his own small business, so there was no parental leave, as such, and never any notion of one of us not working. I accepted an illustration assignment from the hospital bed—I am slightly ashamed to admit that the minute they whisked Tug away to do Medical Stuff to her I asked for my phone so I could check my email. This isn't because I'm an obsessive or especially hard worker—I'm not—but it's just ingrained to me to always be available to clients, because when you're not, they stop asking for you. The upside here is that there was never a painful transition back into the work world, and I never had to fight for a pump room or any of the other things working moms have to do. The downside is that getting anything done was *hard*.

When Tug was tiny we tried to switch off parenting duties as equitably as we could. Lucky for us, she slept a lot as a newborn, but we still felt crunched for time in a way we never had before. (I look back at my pre-Tug self and wonder how I ever had the gall to say I was busy.) It was obvious we would need help. Daycare was more attractive to us than a nanny for a number of reasons—a third adult in the house would have been ridiculous, and if we were home it would have been hard on all of us to be unavailable to the baby. I also liked the idea of her being around other kids, getting socialized. But mostly, money was the big deciding factor.

Our block, oddly enough, has four daycare facilities on it. We went for the cheapest one—a storefront with sun-faded, blind-looking stuffed animals in the window, run by no-nonsense Russians. We were pleasantly surprised when we visited; despite the grim exterior the place was warm and cozy, full of toys and happy-seeming children. We were put on a waiting list in November, and got a slot in May, and called ourselves lucky we had such a short wait. That's New York for you.

It's turned out pretty great, happily. We started Tug at fifteen hours a week and slowly crept up to thirty—those fifteen hours seemed so luxurious at first, but how quickly we filled them! Tug loves her Russian overlords and they seem fond of her; when she was going through a kind of aggressive phase as a young toddler, the owner told me: "She has no fear. What she want, she take. Biggest boy, doesn't matter. She's a monster." I swear I saw a glint of pride in the owner's eyes. Somewhat disconcertingly, however, over a recent long weekend Tug started weeping and asked to "go home." "But you are home," I replied, perplexed. "No! HOME!" "Oh, do you mean daycare?" "YES!!!" I don't expect we can compete with a roomful of toys and a bunch of other kids to play with, but home?? At least she has not, to the best of my knowledge, called any of the Russians Mama yet.

NANNY REJECTS

HAD A BIT OF A METH VIBE

SEEMED UNUSUALLY CONVERSANT IN SEX-TRAFFICKING PRACTICES

THINKS YOU'RE GOING TO HELL

TOO FUCKABLE

GROUP DAYCARE: *Is it for you?*

PRO: EARLY EXPOSURE TO OTHER CULTURES GIVES A CHILD A HEAD START IN ACQUIRING A SECOND LANGUAGE

CON: CHILD AUTOMATICALLY BECOMES VECTOR FOR DISEASE

PRO: CHILD LEARNS SOCIAL SKILLS THAT WILL PROVE INVALUABLE WHEN HE REACHES SCHOOL AGE

CON: GOD ONLY KNOWS HOW THEY REALLY DEAL WITH ALL THOSE TODDLERS

KINGCHESTER MONTESSORI
PRESCHOOL EVALUATION

NAME: Branwyn Z. Adams-Wright

GENDER: (PHYSICAL): M /(F)

GENDER (EXPRESSED): M /(F) (Roughly 890%)

LANGUAGES SPOKEN: English and a
 language she insists is "Fairy-elf giraffe-ish"

HAND DOMINANCE: L /(R)/ Prefers not to use hands

GROSS MOTOR COORDINATION: Branwyn walks with a smooth, rolling gait.
When tested on the "Think 'n' Play", she proved capable of climbing but
unsure of how to extract herself from the 3D rope puzzle. When asked
to do a set of jumping jacks, Branwyn tried to show me her underwear.

SMALL MOTOR COORDINATION: Branwyn was given a selection of sensory toys:
sand, clay, Play-Doh. She was adept at rolling the Play-Doh in the sand
to make "cookies" (NOTE: Branwyn's mother claims that cookies are not permitted
in their house). Branwyn's clay structures, while formally bold, lack narrative cohesion.

Branwyn is able to use a fork and spoon unassisted. However, she announced that
the braised endives and boiled snapper she was served were "yucky."

PERCEPTUAL DEVELOPMENT AND CONCEPTUAL SKILLS: Branwyn grasped the concept
of a 12-piece wooden puzzle, but quickly lost interest in completing it. When
presented with a different puzzle, Branwyn asked if the school had Minecraft
(NOTE: Branwyn's mother claims that Minecraft is not permitted in their home).

Branwyn is able to recognize her own name when written, but insists that her name
is "Princess Pony Farts." When asked if "Princess Pony Farts" is an appropriate
name, Branwyn replied, "You said farts!" and laughed uncontrollably.

When asked which was her right hand, Branwyn shouted "RED" and fell to the floor.

While able to name the letters of the Roman Alphabet, Branwyn seemed
completely unfamiliar with Cyrillic, Arabic, Korean, and Bengali.

Branwyn was unable to describe the shape, color, or taste of anxiety.

EMOTIONAL DEVELOPMENT: Branwyn was presented with the "sad doll." When asked why the doll was sad, Branwyn replied that the doll had drunk too much whiskey (NOTE: Branwyn's mother insists that whiskey is not allowed in their home, at least not during hours when Branwyn is likely to be awake). When asked again, Branwyn claimed that the doll "had the farts." Upon being chided for over-reliance on the word "farts," Branwyn became quiet and said that the doll was sad because its father didn't love it (NOTE: while plausible, this is incorrect; the doll is sad because it cannot have a pet dog). When asked what she might do to cheer the doll up, Branwyn replied, "spank her until I stop crying like a baby."

INTERACTION WITH OTHER CHILDREN: When introduced to her peer group, Branwyn asked if she could stay in a cubby. When told it was time to play with the other children, Branwyn experienced a meltdown and requested that "Nanny Red" come get her (NOTE: as per Mrs. Adams-Wright, Nanny Red is the day nanny). Despite her initial shyness, Branwyn was quite physically aggressive, claiming that "Nanny Red said to fight the biggest one first." When asked to share, Branwyn yelled "SNATCHPOPS" and took Alessandra's cheddar bunnies. During trust games, she let Henry fall to the floor and laughed at him.

PARENTAL INVOLVEMENT: I noted that Branwyn's mother was the only parent present for today's evaluation. I enquired after Branwyn's father; Mrs. Adams-Wright said that Mr. Adams-Wright had to work today. While every family prioritizes things differently, it is worth noting that Branwyn's father seems to place education on a priority level that is perhaps inconsistent with the Montessori ethos. Mrs. Adams-Wright made repeated attempts to contact her husband via cell; it is worth noting that Mr. Adams-Wright seems to take a lot of meetings. Branwyn noted that "Mommy-nanny Red" had wanted to come, but that Mrs. Adams-Wright said no.

SUMMARY NOTES: While I do not feel that Branwyn is yet ready to join the Montessori preschool community, I would be happy to recommend her for the Montessori Basement Remedial Morning Program. Mrs. Adams-Wright assures us that we will have the $500.00 application fee and a deposit of $8000.00 towards tuition by Monday.

PARENTING PHILOSOPHIES

TIGER MOM

PROS: CHILD WILL BE FOCUSED AND ACCOMPLISHED.
CONS: NON-ASIAN CHILDREN ALMOST CERTAIN
TO CRUMBLE UNDER PRESSURE

FRENCH

PROS: CHILD WILL BE INDEPENDENT
AND A SOPHISTICATED EATER
CONS: RUNS THE RISK OF LIKING JERRY
LEWIS AND BEING MEAN TO ALGERIANS

RADICAL UNSCHOOLING

PROS: SAVES EVERYONE THE HASSLE
OF DEALING WITH THE MAN
CONS: MAY REBEL BY JOINING THE TEA PARTY

FERAL

PROS: CHILD UNDERFOOT LESS; WILL MAKE
FASCINATING STUDY IN LATE LANGUAGE ACQUISITION
CONS: VERY LIKELY TO BITE

MOM SHAMERS: A Rogue's Gallery

MY HEART JUST HURTS FOR THOSE BABES LEFT TO CRY ALL ALONE IN A CRIB—

THE SMUG CO-SLEEPER

IT TOOK ME WEEKS TO GET BACK INTO SHAPE AFTER I GAVE BIRTH. WEEKS!

SO... DOES YOUR GYM NOT HAVE A CHILD-WATCH SERVICE?

THE LULULEMON YOGA FIEND

WELL, WE'RE STILL BREAST-FEEDING, SO I'D JUST FEEL WAY TOO GUILTY IF I HAD A GLASS OF WINE.

AND DON'T GET ME STARTED ON COFFEE.

THE TEETOTALING MARTYR

OH, YOU LET HER GO DOWN FACE-FIRST? YOU'RE SO BRAVE.

THIS CUNT

"That Baby Needs A Hat."

I live close to a sizable Caribbean community. If there is one thing a Caribbean lady cannot stand, it's a baby without a hat on. Once the temperature dips below, say, seventy, the sight of an uncovered baby head is like Kryptonite. The tongue-lashing I've received for exposing my daughter's scalp to the breeze is nothing compared to the looks I've gotten when, in winter, I went out with her in a carrier, a bear suit, and yes, a hat—but left her wrists exposed. The glares, the sucked-in breath, the subtle shakes of the head. Yikes.

However. I'll take an honest expression of disapproval any day over the smug, passive-aggressive mom-shaming bullshit that goes on every day on the playground and in the comments sections of every parenting blog. When my daughter was about eighteen months, she loved to slide down the baby slide headfirst. Note that I said baby slide—it's two feet off the ground, and slopes gently to a drop of about four inches, with a long flat runway. You would have to fling a baby onto it to hurt her. Nonetheless: "You're so brave," another mom sniffed, cutting her eyes at me, "letting her do that. I would never be able to let my daughter do such a thing." And heaven help you if you feed a baby formula in public. Or fail to quarter its grapes. Etc. Nobody gives side-eye like a Brooklyn mom these days.

There are gracious ways to respond to this, I'm sure. There's got to be a middle ground between red-faced consternation and stammering out a lame justification (my usual MO) and letting fly a "mind your own fucking business, you miserable cunt" (which is what I say later, in my head). Southern ladies are wonderful at this sort of thing—they can take each other down with an exchange of insults so politely rendered, so dripping with honey, that an outsider might be lulled into thinking the women are dear friends exchanging compliments, not battle-scarred warriors stabbing each other in the heart. Sadly for me, I am not skilled in this particular set of social graces. Living in cities my entire adult life has given me the ability to reply loudly and colorfully to the rando shouting things from his car or on the street, but to effectively shut down a bitchy mom to her face without getting eighty-sixed forever from the neighborhood at large? That's ninja-level shit.

Like a lot of people, I'm pretty conflict-averse. This has nothing to do with being a good person and much more to do with vestiges of being a "nice girl." In the rare instances where I know, unequivocally, that I am IN THE RIGHT, my desire to fight it out, to really mix some shit up, comes singing out of me like a surge of joy. Finally! Finally I get to hand somebody their ass! This isn't a good look for playgroup. However, when people insist on not minding their own business—and it happens quite a lot—perhaps it's time to lay aside a bit of politesse. That nice-girl veneer isn't really serving you much anyway, except to ensure that you remain awkwardly flustered while some mom in nicer shoes than yours throws shade on your parenting skills. Unless you're lucky enough to have earned your patch in the aforementioned Southern social arena or are so badass that nobody would think of coming at you with this nonsense, maybe it's time to get a little blunt. Perhaps a neutral, friendly "Uh-huh—how about you raise your kid, and I'll raise mine?" Something not quite a gauntlet, but that sends an unmistakable MYOB. Something where the "c"-word is implied, not hurled. If you think of anything, please let me know.

TODDLERHOOD

As I write this, my daughter is two. When I started work on this book, she was a completely different kind of creature, and when the book is published, she will be a different creature still. I don't entirely remember what it was like to have an infant. When I hold very young babies, I have to think, Wait, can they hold their head up at this age? Good God, they're floppy—I have memories, of course, of holding tiny New Tug, of putting chubby Six-Month Tug down to sleep, of watching wobbly Year-Old Tug cruise around our living room on thick but unsteady legs, but I don't remember exactly what that was *like*.

It makes me sad to think these Toddler Tug days might recede into a similar mist. I *like* her so very much. I would not describe these days as easy, per se—there are tantrums, there is an obsessive need to watch *Peppa Pig*, there is the constant vigilance required to keep her from splitting her own head open—but she's *fun*. And she's *funny*. The moments of progression and discovery at this age are more interesting and pleasurable—for me, anyway—than any since I got to watch her knitting together in the womb. She's becoming a person, a person who says thank you when you hand her a bottle and likes to be swung from my hands like I'm a trapeze and has a weird Cockney accent sometimes—she says "OUT-SOOOIIIIIDE!" when she wants to go outside, sounding like Drusilla in *Buffy the Vampire Slayer*. ("Spoooiiike!" Am I right?) I liked having a baby when she was one, but babies are, unless you're a serious Baby Person, a bit boring. They certainly can't ask you to draw a letter "P" over and over or cheekily try to lick your belly, which is Tug's favorite new joke. We're just getting started on this whole two-year-old business; maybe by the time she's four or five I'll wonder how in the hell I thought two was any fun at all, what with the peeing on the floor and the flailing and screaming because I won't let her commune with her pink Pig God. Or maybe by the time she's four or five she'll have figured out how to articulate exactly why she despises me, and I will long for the days when she couldn't exactly talk.

Your mileage, of course, may vary. I mentioned these feelings to a mom on the playground with a similarly aged kid and she sighed that she longed for the days before her son became mobile. Which I understand—I never realized quite how easy it was to just *put* Tug somewhere, and she had to *stay* there, because she didn't know how to move yet. I didn't realize that this was easy at the time, because I was too busy worrying that she would randomly die for no reason at all. Now that she can move around, I *know* the reasons she might die, which, while harrowing in their own right, at least have the advantage of being logical. But when I think of her being a big girl—a girl whose feet I won't get to nibble on, 'cause ewwwww,

Mooooommmmm!—I think the Tug I'll miss won't be the roly-poly, cooing, placid Baby Tug, though that Tug was delicious. It'll be the flailing, laughing, hopping, screaming, fit-throwing, kiss-giving, ticklish Toddler Tug, who still giggles when I pretend to eat her feet.

But I'm not going to miss this new psychotic insistence on only wearing purple shirts. That shit is *already* old.

CHILDREN'S PROGRAMMING

SURVIVOR: UNSUPERVISED PLAYGROUND

JUNIOR CROSSFIRE

E-Z RIDER!

FUZZY CLOSE-UP OF A BOOBIE,
TWENTY-FOUR HOURS A DAY

TOYS for THRIFTY PARENTS

CARDBOARD BOXES

WHATEVER YOU CAN STEAL FROM THE LIBRARY

IMAGINATION!

FUCK IT, JUST GO INTO DEBT

TOYCORP.COM

Welcome to the ToyCorp Safety Site! Here you will find tips for safe play, information about products that have been recalled for failure to meet national standards for safety, hygiene, or ethics, and our panic hotline.

The StoryTime Snuggabed is coated with a proprietary substance intended to help children ages 1-3 stay asleep. Consumers reported that children experienced dreams of "a big woof" who told them to "steal Daddy's eyes." Parents whose children are experiencing this phenomenon are instructed to burn the SnuggaBed. Instructions for a ritual burning can be obtained by calling 3-1-1.

ToyCorp has received reports that the GoGoBaby Stroller Entertainment System's DVD player component picks up unwanted transmissions. Should your player display a grainy image of a man speaking Russian, please return the item immediately to ToyCorp. Do not attempt to have the speech translated. Mention this occurrence to no one.

Bundle-Up Snowsuit Sleeper has been found to be made almost entirely of hantavirus. Please contact your local branch of the CDC to arrange an appointment with a hazmat team.

 TuffBabies Stabbin' Set Knife StabToy has been recalled due to stabbing activity.

Customers report several incidents of "spontaneous sentient activity" in models E9J562 and E9J563 of the Lindy Lu Wets-a-Lot Doll. If such activity occurs, locate the white label under the doll's left arm. The label displays the doll's serial number, manufacture date, batch number, and a brief incantation. Reading all of this information aloud will remove the soul from the Doll, which should subsequently be buried in a leach-proof container, well away from the home.

 Due to manufacturing problems, the EnviroSafe Baby Bubble Play Environment renders itself inoperable once the safety latch is locked. Unfortunately, this results in a permanant installation of your child within the Play Environment. ToyCorp will send tutors to educate your child through the secondary level.

The Little Man fedora makes your baby look like an asshole. Please return your hat to ToyCorp for a full refund.

For more information on our products, please contact our Customer Service Professionals by phone (secure landline only, please) or Ouija board.

TODDLER PROTEST METHODS

PASSIVE RESISTANCE

HUNGER STRIKE

STREET THEATER

BOBBY SANDS-STYLE SHIT MANDALA

OTHER PEOPLE'S CHILDREN

ALLERGIC TO NUTS, WHEAT, CERTAIN TONES OF VOICE

NOT ALLOWED TO PLAY WITH KIDS WHO WEREN'T BREASTFED

NOT TO BE TOLD OF EXISTENCE OF SCREENS

PERMITTED TO BREAST FEED FROM ANY LACTATING WOMAN

Saved by
ROCK AND ROLL

I got a gift from the Internet recently. A song I'd seen performed live had been stuck in my head on and off for twenty-one years without my knowing its name. It turns out I had been mistaken about the band—the show was in 1993; I misremembered the opening band and had been barking up the wrong tree in trying to find the song—a mistake easily corrected once it occurred to me how easily it could be found by consulting the hive-mind of Facebook. The song was located, was purchased digitally, and has been on repeat through my headphones for days now. So it goes, nowadays.

Of course, it's not just about the song.* Listening to this scrap of history that finally made its way back to me reminds me of how I used to listen to music—obsessively, and, with certain tracks, almost religiously. I didn't just want to *hear* certain songs, I wanted to be *annihilated* by them. It was a very physical thing to me, then; it ran on a parallel track to sex but was not quite the same thing. I was never in a band so I have no idea what

---

* Shudder to Think, "Lies About the Sky," if you're interested.

it's like, but watching the three or four people up onstage move together in service to this thing, this sound—it felt like they were being ridden by the songs, driven by the spirit, and as a fan with no musical talent, the best I could do was to go home and pick up the needle and play the song over, and over, and over.

And of course sex was involved. The physicality of it wasn't a sexual heat, exactly, but I did want my hands on the bodies of the men making the music. Whatever was riding them, I wanted to be ridden by it too, through any sense possible. I made do with mosh pits, as far as that went. It felt appropriate—the sense was one of wanting to be taken physically, whatever that might mean. I wanted *bruises*.

Fast-forward to my adult life. Those fires have been tamped down in some places and redirected in others. Unlike everything else I was listening to at the time, this song hasn't followed me through the intervening years—it's like a time capsule, a little hit of unadulterated sixteen-year-old-ness. Everything is dead serious when you're sixteen. I'm reminded of the last scene in *Peter and Wendy*, when Peter comes to collect Wendy, who is all grown up:

"Hullo, Peter," she replied faintly, squeezing herself as small as possible. Something inside her was crying, "Woman, woman, let go of me."

That thing is inside me too, and the song woke it up. And here's the thing: I think, before you have kids, you can pretend a little that you might still be able to fly. Once you have kids, you *know* you can't, not anymore. I wouldn't trade my daughter or my life now for anything in the world, but living inside the songs from when I was young—that dangerous, all-consuming desire—that's a different kind of alive. It's powerful, and if you're lucky you've learned how to bank that power a little, to harness it in the service of something creative, maybe. Youthful intensity of feeling is not compatible with the demands of parenthood. You have to be careful, when you go poking around—it can be dangerous to remember that there was a time where you would happily throw yourself on a pyre and burn as brightly as you could.

HALLOWEEN IDEAS

BABY F.D.R.

THE LITTLEST C.H.U.D.

BABY HUMAN CENTIPEDE

MASTER BLASTER

BABY vs. MONKEY

"TEE-HEE! YOU'RE NEVER GONNA WANT TO GO TO COLLEGE!"

POINT FOR MONKEY: WILL STAY CUTE INSTEAD OF GROWING SURLY AND UNGRATEFUL AND DEMANDING TO BORROW THE CAR

"WHY DID YOU PUT ME IN THIS TERRIBLE HOME?"

POINT FOR BABY: EVEN IF THE MONKEY LIVES FOREVER, IT WILL NOT CARE FOR YOU IN YOUR OLD AGE

THBBT-

POINT FOR BABY: NOT CO-ORDINATED ENOUGH TO THROW OWN SHIT* NO MATTER HOW ANGRY

* UNTIL AGE TWO

IT WAS CHEAPER TO CONCEIVE AND BEAR A HUMAN CHILD THAN TO LEGALLY ADOPT A MONKEY.

PLUS SHE'S A LOT LESS LIKELY TO RIP OFF MY FACE.

AND, OF COURSE-

THE PART WITHOUT ANY JOKES

I think about death all the time now. Not in a particularly morbid way, just in a way that the idea of death is always there, hovering over everything. Maybe it would be better to say that the idea of impermanence suffuses my life; I remember as a young teenager, in the middle of some very happy moment—galloping a horse at the stable I worked at, floating in the reservoir we used to sneak into to swim—I would be very aware that this pleasant activity would shortly be the memory of a pleasant activity. I did not, at that age, extrapolate that thought to my eventual death, but I sure do now. At the height of my pleasure in my daughter, there is a thread of feeling that I brought her here without her permission, to hopefully suffer not too much, and certainly to die someday. When I look at her dear, dear tiny face, her round baby cheeks, her bright baby eyes, I am aware that those cheeks will melt into a child's face, which will melt into a young woman's and then an old woman's, and then a dead woman's.

And that's if we're all lucky.

When I say I think about death all the time, I don't mean to say that I brood on it. Sometimes the knowledge that nothing lasts forever is comforting. Sometimes it's terrifying—I don't want to die, I don't want my family to die, and yet, we will. What it is more than anything is puzzling. Why does everything want to live so badly, if it has to die in the end?

Shortly before I got pregnant with my daughter, friends of mine lost their toddler. While I was pregnant, another set of friends delivered at twenty-four weeks; their son died shortly after being born. A week after I gave birth, a third set of friends had to terminate a much-wanted pregnancy. Concrete evidence, really, that the air is full of bullets, and every day you dodge one is a good day.

I believe in God, and the only explanation I can come up with for this is that God doesn't differentiate much between dead and alive. I attend an Episcopalian church because I enjoy it and I want our daughter to grow up with a tradition, but my own admittedly shaky beliefs hew closer to the hippie-dippy notion of a God as an unknowable source. I have to believe that the thing that makes us *us* goes back to that source when our bodies give out, that nothing is ever truly destroyed. But evidence points to that source being largely indifferent to the impermanent, be it pain, or suffering, or joy and physical abundance.

We could sit here and get super-high and talk about the illusory nature of reality, drawing back the veil, and so on, but what I'm learning is this: that loving anything or anyone this much requires you to hold conflicting thoughts in your head and heart. I want to look at her dear,

dear little face forever; nothing lasts forever. It is of the utmost importance that I keep her alive; everyone must die. I will die, her father will die, my little family that is the whole heart of me is the tiniest of tiny blips in the sweep of space and time. We are nothing. We are part of something so grand we cannot hope to apprehend it. We are all lost. We are all floating in space. We were never lost. We will go home. My daughter, my husband, my heart, my loves, my life. I love you so much, and I hope, I hope, I hope.